Amsco's Virginia: Preparing for the SOL Geometry Test

Helen Benyard Luster
Mathematics Teacher
I. C. Norcom High School
Portsmouth, Virginia

Lorenza Luster
Mathematics Consultant
Chesapeake, Virginia

AMSCO SCHOOL PUBLICATIONS, INC.
315 Hudson Street, New York, N. Y., 10013

I would like to dedicate this book to all of the students who are preparing themselves to meet the challenge of the Geometry Standards of Learning Test. I hope that it will give each of you the confidence, skills, and techniques necessary to successfully pass the test. I also dedicate this book to Fernando M. Winnegan, who encouraged me to become a writer; Marcella F. McNeil; my husband, Lorenza O. Luster; and my mother, Ruthie Perry Benyard.

Helen Benyard Luster

This author is presently a math teacher at I. C. Norcom High School in Portsmouth, Virginia. She has taught mathematics for 30 years, the past 28 years in Portsmouth. Her experience includes teaching all levels of mathematics, from basic math to advanced placement calculus. She has served in several leadership positions including Mathematics Department Chairperson, facilitator for staff development, chairperson for curriculum development and coordinator for the development of district level assessment in Algebra and Geometry. She has also presented mathematics workshops at professional conferences at local, state, and national levels. Additionally, she has served as a reader/reviewer for the draft Algebra Instructional Modules for the Virginia Department of Education. She is the co-author of the teaching lesson "Let There Be Light," connecting Math and Biology (through a grant from the Virginia State Department of Education), and is the author of *Virginia: Preparing for the SOL Algebra I Test*. Mrs. Luster has taught the Hands-On Equation Learning System Course (Making Algebra Child's Play) to upper elementary and middle school teachers and was the co-teacher of Measurement and Geometry Standards of Learning for Upper Elementary School Teachers. Mrs. Luster is a member of the TCTM, VCTM, WME, and NCTM.

Reviewers:
Dennis Adkins   **Susan Proffitt**

Text Composition and Artwork: Nesbitt Graphics, Inc.
Cover Design by: A Good Thing, Inc.

Geometry Standards of Learning copyright © 2002 by the Commonwealth of Virginia Department of Education.
All rights reserved. Reprinted with permission.

For additional information contact:

Virginia Department of Education, Division of Instruction at
http://www.pen.k12.va.us/VDOE/Instruction,
or P.O. Box 2120, Richmond, VA 23218-2120

Please visit our Web site at:

www.amscopub.com

When ordering this book please specify: either **R 784 W** or
VIRGINIA: PREPARING FOR THE SOL GEOMETRY TEST

ISBN 1-56765-563-7

Contents

UNIT 1 Lines and Angles

UNIT 2 Triangles and Logic

UNIT 3   Polygons and Circles

UNIT 4   Three-Dimensional Figures

UNIT 5   Coordinate Relations and Transformations

Sample Tests

Index

General Information

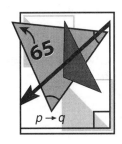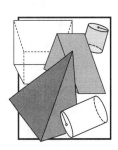

Introduction

The Standard of Learning (SOL) test for Geometry will have a major impact on how Geometry is taught and learned in the state of Virginia. This book is intended for students who are preparing to take the Geometry End of Course Test and for teachers to use as a teaching tool. It is based on the fourteen Geometry objectives, which are divided into five reporting categories. These reporting categories are Lines and Angles; Triangles and Logic; Polygons and Circles; Three-Dimensional Figures; and Coordinate Relations and Transformations. The practice book matches particular objectives to each of the categories.

The book begins with a full-length Diagnostic Test. An Answer Key for this test is provided, along with a mapping chart to help the students identify their strengths and weaknesses in each reporting category. The mapping chart can be used to develop a plan of study.

The practice lessons give a step-by-step review of the types of problems that might occur on the Virginia End-of-Course Exam in Geometry. In addition to the review examples, there are open-ended problems to try and sample multiple-choice questions to solve similar to the format used on the Virginia End-of-Course Exam in Geometry.

Facts About the Geometry Examination

The Geometry Standard of Learning test is an untimed multiple-choice item test consisting of four answer choices for each question. Students are given ancillary materials such as rulers, scratch paper, protractors, compass, patty paper, a formula sheet, and a graphing calculator (Casio or Texas Instrument).

Helpful Hints For the Student

- Answer every question. There is no penalty for incorrect answers on the test. First, answer all the easy questions. Then tackle the hard ones. Do not get bogged down on any one question and do not rush. Eliminate as many wrong answers as you can. If you do not understand a question, circle that question and go to the next question. You will be able to go back to that question later.

- Be careful not to make any stray marks on your answer sheet. The test is machine scanned and you do not want the machine to pick up the wrong answer. Check frequently to make sure that you are answering the question in the correct location on the answer sheet. It is very easy to mark the wrong answer space. You are allowed to write in your test book. You will also be given scratch paper to write on.

- Before the test, do your best to learn the geometry that will be on the test. Take the Diagnostic Test and score the test so that you will have a record of the skills that you need to review and practice before the actual test. First, concentrate on the skills that you need to practice, meaning the skills that you missed on the Diagnostic Test. Next, review the skills that you got correct, and finally, take Sample Tests A, B, and C.

- Be sure that you know the features of the calculator that you are using. Remember, before taking the SOL test, the memory of the calculator will be erased. So do not practice with any written programs.

Diagnostic Test   Take the Diagnostic Test and evaluate your performance on skills that will be tested on the SOL Algebra Test. After you have completed the Diagnostic Test, identify the specific practices that need improvement.

Diagnostic Test

Directions: *Each of the questions or statements below is followed by four suggested answers. Choose the one that is best in each case. You are permitted to use a graphing calculator, a compass, a straightedge, patty paper, scratch paper and a formula sheet. Please use the answer sheet on page xv to record your answers. The formula sheet can be found on page 215.*

1. What is the value of x?

   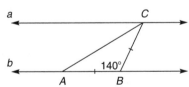

   A 5

   B 20

   C 30

   D 43

2. The supplement of an angle is three times as large as the angle. Find the measure of the angle.

   F 45°

   G 60°

   H 69°

   J 135°

3. **Given:** $\overline{AB} \cong \overline{BC}$ and m$\angle ABC = 140°$.

   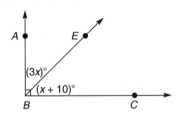

   What is the measure of $\angle CAB$?

   A 10°

   B 20°

   C 40°

   D 140°

4. Given $\angle NOP$, construct $\angle PON'$ with $\angle NOP \cong \angle PON'$.

   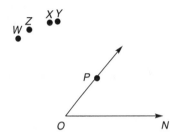

   Which point does the construction of $\angle PON'$ pass through?

   F W

   G X

   H Y

   J Z

5. Which pair of angles must be congruent in order for $\overline{OR}$ to be parallel to $\overline{TP}$?

   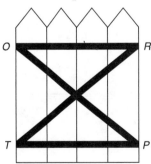

   A $\angle POR$ and $\angle ORP$

   B $\angle POR$ and $\angle RTP$

   C $\angle RTP$ and $\angle TPO$

   D $\angle POR$ and $\angle TPO$

6. **Given:** $a \parallel b$ and $m\angle 1 = 55°$.

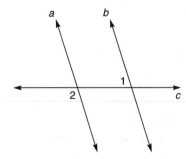

What is the measure of $\angle 2$?

F 45°

G 65°

H 100°

J 125°

7. **Given:** $A(1, 1)$, $B(3, 4)$ and $D(7, 4)$.

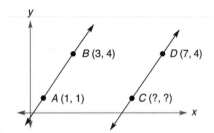

Which coordinates for C make $\overline{AB} \parallel \overline{DC}$?

A (5, 1)

B (5, 2)

C (5, 4)

D (6, 1)

8. Find the value of x that makes $a \parallel b$.

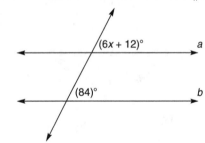

F 12

G 13

H 14

J 16

9. Which pair of lines are parallel?

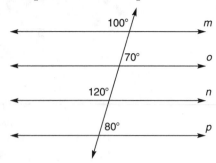

A m and o

B m and p

C n and p

D o and n

10.

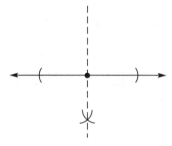

The drawing shows the arcs for a construction of —

F an angle bisector

G a perpendicular to a line from a point not on the line

H a perpendicular to a line from a point on the line

J a perpendicular bisector

11. Which point lies on the angle bisector of $\angle ABC$?

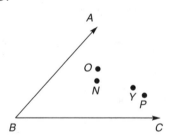

A N

B O

C P

D Y

12. Which is the converse of the statement, "If two angles are congruent, then they are vertical angles"?

  F If two angles are not congruent, then they are not vertical angles.

  G If two angles are vertical angles, then they are congruent.

  H If two angles are not vertical angles, then they are congruent.

  J If two angles are vertical angles, then they are not congruent.

13. Which conclusion logically follows the true statements?

  $p \rightarrow b$

  $\sim a \rightarrow \sim b$

  A $p \rightarrow \sim b$

  B $p \rightarrow \sim a$

  C $p \rightarrow a$

  D $a \rightarrow p$

14. Based on the Venn diagram below, which statement is true?

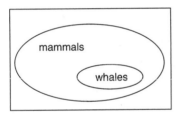

  F No mammals are whales.

  G No whales are mammals.

  H All mammals are whales.

  J All whales are mammals.

15. Let p represent "$\overline{AB} \perp \overline{BC}$."
  Let q represent "$\angle ABC$ is a right angle."
  Which represents the contrapositive of "If $\overline{AB} \perp \overline{BC}$, then $\angle ABC$ is a right angle"?

  A $q \rightarrow p$

  B $q \rightarrow \sim p$

  C $\sim q \rightarrow p$

  D $\sim q \rightarrow \sim p$

16. **Given:** $m\angle A = 60°$ and $m\angle B = 55°$.

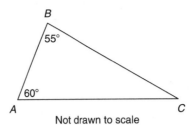

Not drawn to scale

  Which lists the lengths of the sides in order from least to greatest?

  F AB, AC, BC

  G AC, AB, BC

  H AC, BC, AB

  J BC, AC, AB

17.

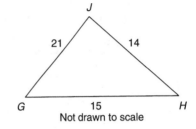

Not drawn to scale

  From smallest to largest, the angles of $\triangle JGH$ are —

  A $\angle G, \angle J, \angle H$

  B $\angle H, \angle G, \angle J$

  C $\angle J, \angle G, \angle H$

  D $\angle J, \angle H, \angle G$

18. If two sides of a triangle have lengths 7 and 11, which is a possible length for the third side of the triangle?

  F 18

  G 5

  H 4

  J 2

19.

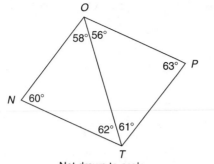

Not drawn to scale

Which is the longest line segment?

A $\overline{NO}$

B $\overline{NT}$

C $\overline{PO}$

D $\overline{TO}$

20. Given: $\overline{AB} \cong \overline{CD}$, and $\angle ABC \cong \angle BCD$.

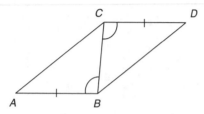

Which could be used to prove $\triangle ABC \cong \triangle DCB$?

F AAS

G HL

H SAS

J ASA

21. Find the height of the tree to the nearest foot.

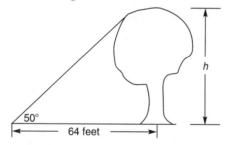

A 39 feet

B 46 feet

C 72 feet

D 76 feet

22. A skating ramp needs to be built at an incline of 30° and at a height of 4 feet.

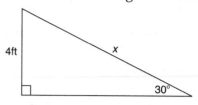

How long is the incline of the skating ramp?

F 4 feet

G $4\sqrt{2}$ feet

H $4\sqrt{3}$ feet

J 8 feet

23. Given: $\angle I \cong \angle M$.

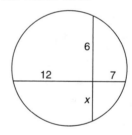

Which could be used to prove $\triangle HJI \sim \triangle KJM$?

A SAS~

B SSS~

C ASA~

D AA~

24. What is the value of x?

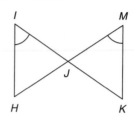

F 13

G 14

H 38

J 78

25. Given: $\square ABCD$ with diagonals $\overline{BD}$ and $\overline{AC}$.

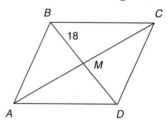

If $BM = 18$, then $BD = \underline{\ ?\ }$.

A 36

B 27

C 18

D 9

26. **Given:** O is the center of the circle.

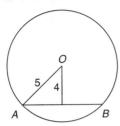

Find the length of $\overline{AB}$.

F 3

G 6

H 8

J 9

27. What is the measure of an interior angle of a regular pentagon?

A 120°

B 108°

C 72°

D 60°

28. If the vertices of quadrilateral $COAT$ are $C(2, 1)$, $O(2, 5)$, $A(6, 5)$, and $T(6, 1)$, then $COAT$ is a —

F rhombus

G rectangle

H square

J trapezoid

29. Find the value of x.

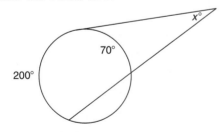

A 60°

B 65°

C 115°

D 135°

30. The tiling pattern below is created using congruent squares and triangles.

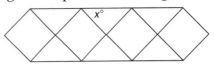

What is the value of x?

F 90°

G 60°

H 45°

J 30°

31. Point A marks the center of the circle.

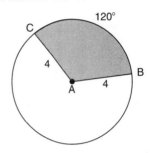

Find the area of the shaded sector.

A $\frac{4}{3}\pi$

B $\frac{8}{3}\pi$

C $\frac{16}{3}\pi$

D $\frac{2}{3}\pi$

32. Given $\overline{TS}$ is tangent to circle O, find the value of x.

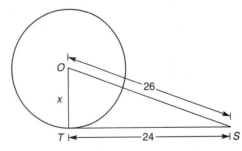

F 2

G 10

H 35

J 100

33. Find the value of x.

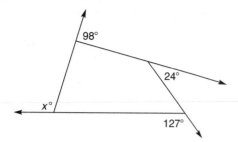

    A 98°
    B 111°
    C 127°
    D 291°

34. Which 2-dimensional pattern can be folded into a cube?

    F
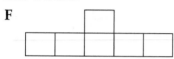

    G
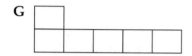

    H
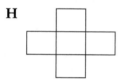

    J
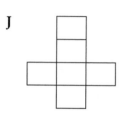

35. What 3-dimensional figure is formed by folding the pattern along the dotted lines?

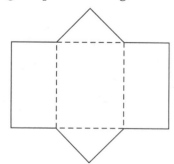

    A Cylinder
    B Triangular prism
    C Rectangular prism
    D Triangular pyramid

36. What is the volume of the figure below?

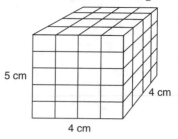

    F 12 cm^3
    G 16 cm^3
    H 80 cm^3
    J 144 cm^3

37. A coffee can takes the shape of a cylinder with a radius of 5 inches and a height of 10 inches.

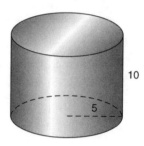

What is the total surface area of the coffee can?
    A 50π in.^{2}
    B 150π in.^{2}
    C 250π in.^{2}
    D 314π in.^{2}

38. The volumes of two similar cones are 8π and 27π cubic units. What is the ratio of the lateral areas of the cones?
    F 2:3
    G 4:9
    H 8:27
    J 16:81

39. If the radius and height of a cone are doubled, then the volume of the cone —
    A increases two times
    B increases four times
    C increases six times
    D increases eight times

40. Given: □*TOCP*.

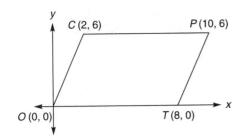

Find *CT*.

F 6.33

G 8.49

H 11.31

J 11.66

41. Which is the front view of the object shown below?

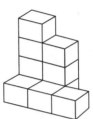

A

B

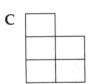

C

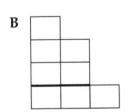

D

42. Which of the figures shows the letter A and its reflection across the *x*-axis?

F

G

H

J

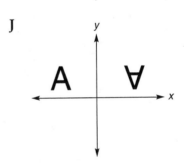

43. △*A′B′C′* is _?_ .

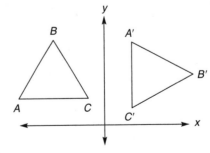

A a rotation of △*ABC* about the origin

B a reflection of △*ABC* across the *x*-axis

C a translation of △*ABC*

D a reflection of △*ABC* across the *y*-axis

44. All the vertices of the rectangle below have integral coordinates.

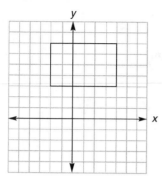

Which pair of points pass through one of the lines of symmetry of the rectangle?

F (⁻4, 5) and (6, 5)

G (⁻3, ⁻4) and (⁻3, 6)

H (0, 0) and (0, 4)

J (1, 2) and (2, ⁻8)

45. The coordinates of the midpoint of $\overline{CD}$ are (4, ⁻5), and the coordinates of C are (8, ⁻8). What are the coordinates of D?

A (⁻2, 0)

B (0, 0)

C (0, ⁻2)

D (2, ⁻2)

Diagnostic Test Answer Sheet

Use a No. 2 pencil. Fill in the circles completely. If you erase, erase completely. Incomplete erasures may be read as answers.

1. Ⓐ Ⓑ Ⓒ Ⓓ

2. Ⓕ Ⓖ Ⓗ Ⓙ

3. Ⓐ Ⓑ Ⓒ Ⓓ

4. Ⓕ Ⓖ Ⓗ Ⓙ

5. Ⓐ Ⓑ Ⓒ Ⓓ

6. Ⓕ Ⓖ Ⓗ Ⓙ

7. Ⓐ Ⓑ Ⓒ Ⓓ

8. Ⓕ Ⓖ Ⓗ Ⓙ

9. Ⓐ Ⓑ Ⓒ Ⓓ

10. Ⓕ Ⓖ Ⓗ Ⓙ

11. Ⓐ Ⓑ Ⓒ Ⓓ

12. Ⓕ Ⓖ Ⓗ Ⓙ

13. Ⓐ Ⓑ Ⓒ Ⓓ

14. Ⓕ Ⓖ Ⓗ Ⓙ

15. Ⓐ Ⓑ Ⓒ Ⓓ

16. Ⓕ Ⓖ Ⓗ Ⓙ

17. Ⓐ Ⓑ Ⓒ Ⓓ

18. Ⓕ Ⓖ Ⓗ Ⓙ

19. Ⓐ Ⓑ Ⓒ Ⓓ

20. Ⓕ Ⓖ Ⓗ Ⓙ

21. Ⓐ Ⓑ Ⓒ Ⓓ

22. Ⓕ Ⓖ Ⓗ Ⓙ

23. Ⓐ Ⓑ Ⓒ Ⓓ

24. Ⓕ Ⓖ Ⓗ Ⓙ

25. Ⓐ Ⓑ Ⓒ Ⓓ

26. Ⓕ Ⓖ Ⓗ Ⓙ

27. Ⓐ Ⓑ Ⓒ Ⓓ

28. Ⓕ Ⓖ Ⓗ Ⓙ

29. Ⓐ Ⓑ Ⓒ Ⓓ

30. Ⓕ Ⓖ Ⓗ Ⓙ

31. Ⓐ Ⓑ Ⓒ Ⓓ

32. Ⓕ Ⓖ Ⓗ Ⓙ

33. Ⓐ Ⓑ Ⓒ Ⓓ

34. Ⓕ Ⓖ Ⓗ Ⓙ

35. Ⓐ Ⓑ Ⓒ Ⓓ

36. Ⓕ Ⓖ Ⓗ Ⓙ

37. Ⓐ Ⓑ Ⓒ Ⓓ

38. Ⓕ Ⓖ Ⓗ Ⓙ

39. Ⓐ Ⓑ Ⓒ Ⓓ

40. Ⓕ Ⓖ Ⓗ Ⓙ

41. Ⓐ Ⓑ Ⓒ Ⓓ

42. Ⓕ Ⓖ Ⓗ Ⓙ

43. Ⓐ Ⓑ Ⓒ Ⓓ

44. Ⓕ Ⓖ Ⓗ Ⓙ

45. Ⓐ Ⓑ Ⓒ Ⓓ

Answers and Analysis Chart

Use the key below to score your Diagnostic Test. Circle the number of any question that you either left blank or answered incorrectly. Study the analysis chart to determine which practice reviews require additional work. Work through those reviews and complete the assessment sections for those practice reviews. It would be beneficial to work though the other practice reviews and assessment sections for a complete review of the topics covered on the Geometry SOL Test.

ANSWER	SOL	PRACTICE	REVIEW PAGES
1. B	G.3	1	1–9
2. F	G.3	1	1–9
3. B	G.3	1	1–9
4. G	G.11	4	22–34
5. D	G.4	3	15–22
6. J	G.3	1	1–9
7. A	G.4	3	15–22
8. F	G.4	3	15–22
9. B	G.4	3	15–22
10. H	G.11	4	22–34
11. A	G.11	4	22–34
12. G	G.1a	6	40–44
13. C	G.1d	8	50–57
14. J	G.1c	8	50–57
15. D	G.1b	7	44–49
16. H	G.6	11	75–78
17. A	G.6	11	75–78
18. G	G.6	11	75–78
19. A	G.6	11	75–78
20. H	G.5b	10	65–74
21. D	G.7	12	79–87
22. J	G.7	12	79–87
23. D	G.5b	10	65–74
24. G	G.10	18	119–131

ANSWER	SOL	PRACTICE	REVIEW PAGES
25. A	G.8a	14	91–98
26. G	G.10	18	119–131
27. B	G.9	17	110–118
28. H	G.8b	15	98–105
29. B	G.10	18	119–131
30. H	G.9	17	110–118
31. C	G.10	18	119–131
32. G	G.10	12	79–87
33. B	G.9	17	110–118
34. J	G.12	20	135–141
35. B	G.12	20	135–141
36. H	G.13	21	141–148
37. B	G.13	21	141–148
38. G	G.14a	22	148–153
39. D	G.14b	22	148–153
40. G	G.2a	24	158–164
41. B	G.12	20	135–141
42. G	G.2c	26	170–178
43. A	G.2c	26	170–178
44. F	G.2b	25	165–169
45. C	G.2a	24	158–164

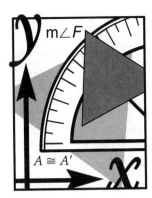

UNIT 1
Lines and Angles

PRACTICE 1   Working with Angles

Objective: **SOL G.3**

❏ The student will solve practical problems involving complementary, supplementary, and congruent angles that include vertical angles, angles formed when parallel lines are cut by a transversal, and angles in polygons.

Parallel Lines and Angles   Study the list below to review some of the basic angle pairs:

- **Congruent angles:** angles that have the same measure.
- **Complementary angles:** two angles that have a sum of 90°.
- **Supplementary angles:** two angles that have a sum of 180°.
- **Vertical angles:** two non-adjacent angles formed by two intersecting lines. These angles are *always* congruent.
- **Linear pair of angles:** two adjacent angles formed by two intersecting lines. These angles are *always* supplementary.

Examples of vertical angles are shown in the figure below on the left: ∠1 and ∠3; ∠2 and ∠4. Examples of linear pairs are shown in the figure below on the left: ∠1 and ∠2; ∠2 and ∠3; ∠3 and ∠4; ∠1 and ∠4.

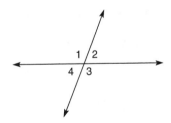

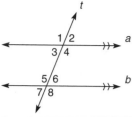

Line *a* is parallel to line *b*.

Use the figure on the left to review pairs of angles formed by a transversal cutting two parallel lines:

- **Alternate interior angles:** $\angle 4$ and $\angle 5$, which lie between the parallel lines on alternate sides of the transversal on different vertices, form this type of angle pair. Since $a \parallel b$, these angles are congruent. Other examples are $\angle 3$ and $\angle 6$.

- **Alternate exterior angles:** $\angle 1$ and $\angle 8$, which lie outside of the parallel lines on alternate sides of the transversal on different vertices, form this type of angle pair. Since $a \parallel b$, these angles are congruent. Other examples are $\angle 2$ and $\angle 7$.

- **Corresponding angles:** $\angle 1$ and $\angle 5$, one of which lies between the parallel lines and the other of which lies outside of the parallel lines, both lying on the same side of the transversal on different vertices, form this type of angle pair. Since $a \parallel b$, these angles are congruent. Other examples are $\angle 3$ and $\angle 7$; $\angle 2$ and $\angle 6$; $\angle 4$ and $\angle 8$.

- **Same-side interior** or **consecutive interior angles:** $\angle 3$ and $\angle 5$, which lie between the parallel lines on the same side of the transversal, form this type of angle pair. Since $a \parallel b$, these angles are supplementary. Other examples are $\angle 4$ and $\angle 6$.

Note: When a transversal cuts two parallel lines, any pair of angles formed is either congruent or supplementary. This is true *only* for parallel lines. In particular, when a transversal cuts two lines that are *not* parallel, the alternate interior, alternate exterior, and corresponding angles are *not* congruent, and the same-side (consecutive) interior angles are *not* supplementary. For example,

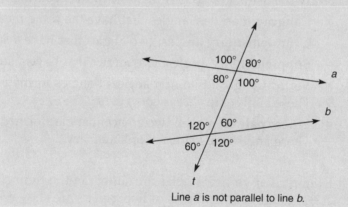

Line *a* is not parallel to line *b*.

Model Problem 1   The complement of an angle is two times as large as the angle. Find the angle.

Solution   Let x be the unknown angle. The complement of an angle means $90° - x$, but we're also told that the complement is $2x$. Set these expressions equal to each other and solve for x.

$$90 - x = 2x$$
$$90 = 3x$$
$$30 = x$$

Therefore, the angle measures $30°$.

Model Problem 2   Given: ∠1 is supplementary to ∠4 and ∠4 is supplementary to ∠5.

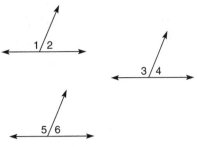

What do you know about the measures of ∠1 and ∠5?

Solution   m∠1 = m∠5, because if two angles are supplementary to two angles with equal measure, then the two angles are congruent. We can prove this algebraically by applying the definition of supplementary angles.

STATEMENTS	REASONS
1. m∠1 + m∠4 = 180 and m∠4 + m∠5 = 180	1. Definition of supplementary angles
2. m∠1 + m∠4 = m∠4 + m∠5	2. Substitution property
3. m∠1 = m∠5	3. Subtract m∠4

Model Problem 3   Find the measure of ∠ADE in the figure below.

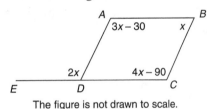

The figure is not drawn to scale.

Solution   Step 1.   Find the value of x.

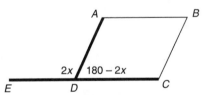

The missing angle ∠ADC is the supplement of ∠ADE since they form a linear pair. This means that their sum is 180° or $2x + $ m∠ADC = 180. Thus, m∠ADC = $180 - 2x$.

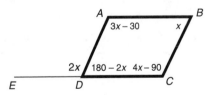

The sum of the interior angles of a quadrilateral is 360°.

Solve for x.

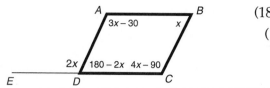

$$(180 - 2x) + (3x - 30) + (x) + (4x - 90) = 360$$
$$(^-2x + 3x + x + 4x) + (180 - 30 - 90) = 360$$
$$6x + 60 = 360$$
$$6x = 300$$
$$x = 50$$

Step 2.   Find the measure of $\angle ADE$.

$$m\angle ADE = 2x = 2 \cdot 50 = 100°$$

Therefore, the measure of $\angle ADE$ is 100°.

Model Problem 4   Find the value of x if $c \parallel d$.

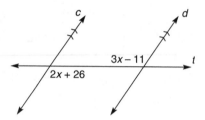

Solution   The given angles are alternate interior angles. When a transversal cuts parallel lines, alternate interior angles are congruent.

$$3x - 11 = 2x + 26$$
$$x = 37$$

Therefore, $x = 37$.

Model Problem 5   If $m\angle 1 = 115°$, then $m\angle 5 = \underline{\ ?\ }$.

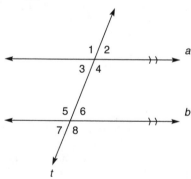

Solution   Angles 1 and 5 are corresponding angles. When a transversal cuts parallel lines, corresponding angles are congruent. Therefore, if $m\angle 1 = 115°$, then $m\angle 5 = 115°$.

Model Problem 6   Find the value of x in the figure below.

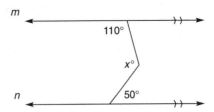

Solution   Step 1.   Through the vertex at x, only one line can be drawn parallel to lines n and m. Draw this line and look for relationships that will help find the value of x.

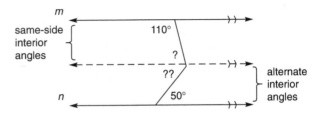

We see that a pair of same-side interior angles and a pair of alternate interior angles are formed.

Step 2.   Find the values of the missing parts of x.

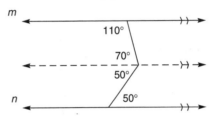

The two same-side interior angles are supplementary (since they are formed by a transversal cutting two parallel lines). Since the sum of supplementary angles is 180°, the top part of x is $180° - 110° = 70°$. Similarly, the two alternate interior angles are congruent. Thus, the other part of x is 50°.

Step 3.   Combine the missing parts. The total value of x is $70° + 50° = 120°$.

Angles of a Polygon

The sum of the interior angles of a polygon can be found by using the formula $(n - 2)180°$, where n represents the number of sides of the particular polygon.

Example: Find the sum of the interior angles in a hexagon.

Solution: Since there are six sides in a hexagon, let $n = 6$, and use the formula.

$$(n - 2)180 = (6 - 2)180 = (4)180 = 720$$

Thus, the sum of the interior angles in a hexagon is 720°.

1. Find the value of x if $l \parallel m$.

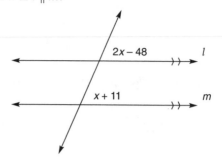

2. **Given:** $\angle ABD$ is a right angle.

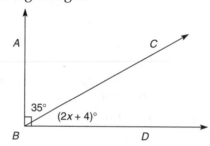

   Find m$\angle CBD$.

3. Find the value of x.

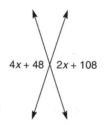

4. Find the measure of $\angle 2$ if $m \parallel n$.

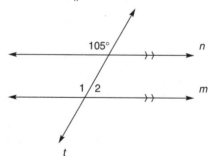

5. Find the value of x.

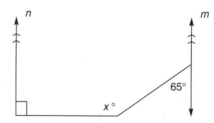

   Hint: Rotate the figure 90° clockwise and follow the steps in Model Problem 6.

6. Find the value of x in the figure below.

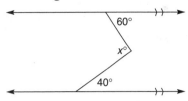

7. **Given:** $c \parallel d$ and $a \parallel b$.

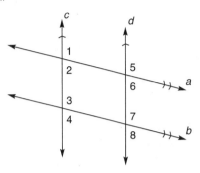

Find the measure of $\angle 7$ if the measure of $\angle 1$ is $141°$.

8. The complement of an angle is $20°$ less than the angle. Find the measure of the angle.

ASSESSMENT

1.

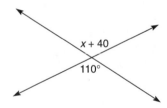

Solve for x.

A 30

B 35

C 50

D 70

2. Find the value of x if $a \parallel b$.

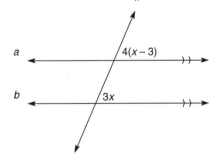

F 3

G 12

H 26.14

J 27.43

3. Which angles are congruent to $\angle 1$ if $a \parallel b$?

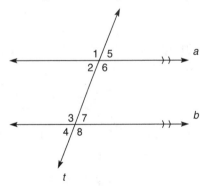

A $\angle 2$, $\angle 6$, and $\angle 8$

B $\angle 3$, $\angle 6$, and $\angle 8$

C $\angle 4$, $\angle 5$, and $\angle 7$

D $\angle 4$, $\angle 6$, and $\angle 8$

4. Find the value of x.

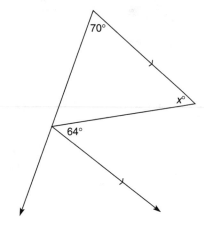

F 134°

G 110°

H 64°

J 46°

5. Find m∠7 if $r \parallel s$ and m∠1 = 58°.

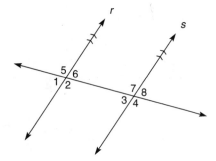

A 32

B 58

C 122

D 148

6. Find the measure of ∠ADE in the figure below.

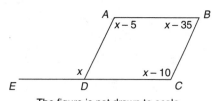

The figure is not drawn to scale.

F 105°

G 115°

H 122.5°

J 147.5°

7. Given: $\overline{AB}$ bisects ∠CAD, m∠CAB = (2x + 4), and m∠BAD = (3x − 19).

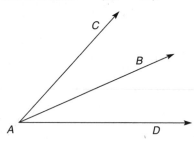

Find m∠BAD.

Note: A ray **bisects** an angle when it divides the given angle into two equal parts.

A 15°

B 23°

C 46°

D 50°

8. Find the value of x if $a \parallel b$ with transversal t.

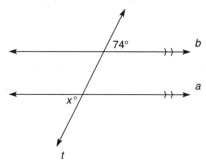

F 164°

G 106°

H 74°

J 54°

9. Find the value of x in the figure below.

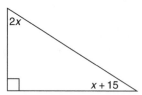

A 15

B 25

C 55

D 75

10. Find the value of x in the figure below.

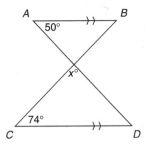

    F 56°

    G 50°

    H 40°

    J 16°

11. The supplement of an angle is twice as large as the angle. Find the measure of the angle.

    A 30°

    B 60°

    C 90°

    D 180°

12. Pentagon *ABCDE* has four congruent angles. Which represents the measure of one of the congruent angles?

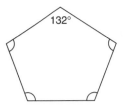

    F 57°

    G 102°

    H 132°

    J 147°

13. Find the measure of ∠1 if it forms a straight angle with ∠20° and ∠125°.

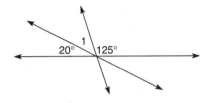

Note: A **straight angle** is an angle with a measure of 180° forming a straight line.

    A 125°

    B 20°

    C 65°

    D 35°

PRACTICE 2   Angles Formed by Parallel Lines and Angles in Polygons

Objective:	SOL G.3

❏ The student will solve practical problems involving complementary, supplementary, and congruent angles that include vertical angles, angles formed when parallel lines are cut by a transversal, and angles in polygons.

REMEMBER

The figures in this book are not always drawn to scale.

This practice will look at real-world examples involving congruent, complementary, or supplementary angles as well as the angles formed when parallel lines are cut by a transversal.

Model Problem 1   Find the value of x.

Solution   The 70° angle and angle x form a pair of supplementary angles with the ground. Since the sum of supplementary angles is 180°, $70 + x = 180$. Solve for x.

$$70 + x = 180$$
$$x = 110$$

Therefore, $x = 110°$.

Model Problem 2   Below is a design of a robotic arm in which $\overline{AB} \parallel \overline{CD}$.

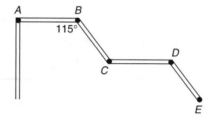

Find the measure of $\angle BCD$ if the measure of $\angle ABC$ is 115°.

Solution

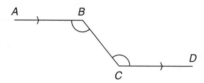

With $\overline{AB} \parallel \overline{CD}$ and using $\overline{BC}$ as the transversal, a pair of alternate interior angles are formed. Use the theorem that states *if two parallel lines are cut by a transversal, then the alternate interior angles are congruent.* Therefore, the measure of $\angle BCD$ is 115°.

Model Problem 3   A bridge has been constructed using a series of congruent equilateral triangles. Find the measure of $\angle 1$.

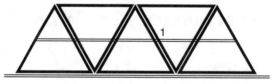

The horizontal beams are parallel.

Solution   Consider only a section of the bridge.

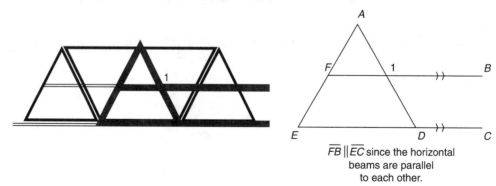

$\overline{FB} \parallel \overline{EC}$ since the horizontal beams are parallel to each other.

Step 1.

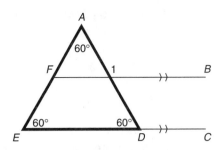

We are told that △ADE is equilateral. In an equilateral triangle, all of the interior angles measure 60°.

Step 2. Let ∠2 represent the angle adjacent to ∠1.

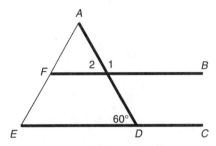

∠2 and ∠ADE form a pair of corresponding angles. Since $\overline{FB} \parallel \overline{EC}$, m∠2 = 60°.

Step 3.

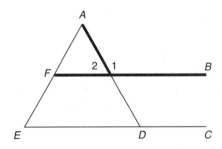

m∠1 + m∠2 = 180, because ∠1 and ∠2 form a linear pair. Replace m∠2 by 60 and solve for x.

$$m\angle 1 + m\angle 2 = 180$$
$$m\angle 1 + 60 = 180$$
$$m\angle 1 = 120°$$

TRY THESE

1. A bird feeder is placed on a board as shown below. If the board is placed parallel to the ground, what is the value of x?

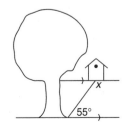

2. A patio has the shape shown below with three of its angles measuring 85°, 94°, and 104°.

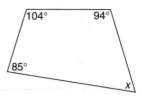

Find the measure of the missing angle, *x*.

For problems 3 and 4, use the figure below.

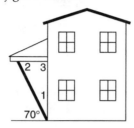

3. The house has a brace on its porch that makes a 70° angle with the ground as shown. Which angle is a complement of the 70° angle?

4. The porch and the ground are parallel to each other. Which angle is congruent to the 70° angle?

5. The front door of a community center is in the shape of a rectangle.

Find the value of *x*.

6. What is the value of *x* in the figure below?

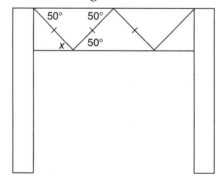

7. The support of a water tower is constructed using shapes of rhombuses and triangles.

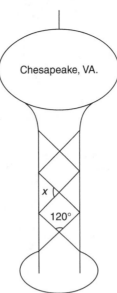

Chesapeake, VA.

x

120°

Find the value of x in degrees.

ASSESSMENT

For problems 1 and 2, use the figure below.

100° 3 4
1   2
ℓ

The figure shows the layout of a parking lot. Line ℓ represents the center curb and the other lines are parallel to each other.

1. Which angle is supplementary to the 100° angle?
    A 1
    B 2
    C 3
    D 4

2. Which angle corresponds to the 100° angle?
    F 1
    G 2
    H 3
    J 4

3. A tree planted in the spring needs braces to help it to grow straight.

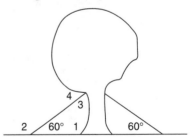

4
3
2   60° 1   60°

The brace makes a 60° angle with the ground. Which angle is supplementary to the 60° angle?

    A 1
    B 2
    C 3
    D 4

4. The figure below represents the doors on Lorenza's storage building with $\overline{AB} \perp \overline{AD}$ and $\overline{AB} \parallel \overline{DC}$.

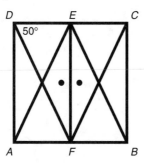

If the measure of $\angle EDF$ is 50°, what is the measure of $\angle ADF$?

F 140°

G 130°

H 50°

J 40°

5. The pattern in Edward's bathroom floor is made with tiles shaped like equilateral triangles. Find the value of x.

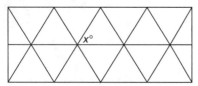

A 30°

B 45°

C 60°

D 90°

6. What is the measure of $\angle 1$ in the figure below?

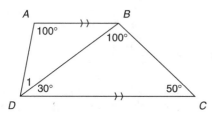

F 80°

G 50°

H 30°

J 20°

7. A house lot is in the shape of the figure below.

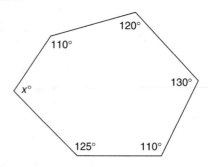

Find the value of x.

A 70°

B 110°

C 125°

D 130°

8. The banister of Carlton's porch is shown below.

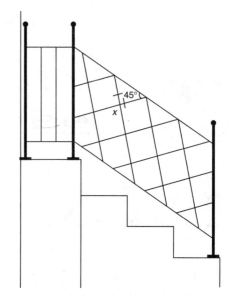

Find the value of x in degrees.

F 45°

G 60°

H 90°

J 135°

9. The body of a crane is in the shape of a hexagon.

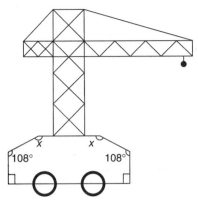

What is the value of x in degrees?

A 80°

B 118°

C 142°

D 162°

10. In order to cut out a regular pentagon from a piece of paper, what should be the measure of each angle of the pentagon?

F 36°

G 72°

H 108°

J 144°

PRACTICE 3   Proving Lines Parallel

Objective:	SOL G.4

☐ The student will use the relationships between angles formed by two lines cut by a transversal to determine if the two lines are parallel and verify, using algebraic and coordinate methods as well as deductive proofs.

The following table contains shortened versions of theorems used to determine when two lines cut by a transversal are parallel.

TYPE OF ANGLES	RELATIONSHIP	CONCLUSION
Corresponding	If congruent, If *not* congruent,	then the two lines are parallel then the two lines are *not* parallel
Alternate interior	If congruent, If *not* congruent,	then the two lines are parallel then the two lines are *not* parallel
Alternate exterior	If congruent, If *not* congruent,	then the two lines are parallel then the two lines are *not* parallel
Same-side (consecutive) interior	If supplementary, If *not* supplementary,	then the two lines are parallel then the two lines are *not* parallel

Model Problem 1   State a postulate or theorem that justifies $a \parallel b$.

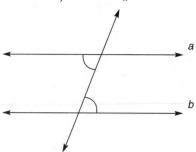

Solution   The marked angles are congruent alternate interior angles. From the table, if two lines are cut by a transversal and alternate interior angles are congruent, then the two lines are parallel.

Model Problem 2   Line ℓ is parallel to line m when the value of x is ___?___ .

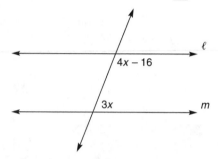

Solution   These are same-side interior angles (also called consecutive interior angles). Lines ℓ and m will be parallel when these types of angles are supplementary. Thus, the sum of the two angles should be 180°.

$$(4x - 16) + 3x = 180$$
$$7x - 16 = 180$$
$$7x = 196$$
$$x = 28$$

Therefore, $x = 28$.

Model Problem 3   The measure of $\angle BAD$ is 45° and the measure of $\angle ABD$ is 30°.

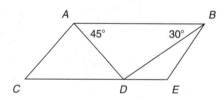

Which of the following angles must also measure 45° in order for $\overline{AB}$ to be parallel to $\overline{CE}$?

Solution   Step 1.   Draw the pair of lines and the transversal that contains the 45° angle.

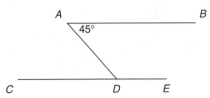

Step 2.   Identify the types of angles formed in the figure

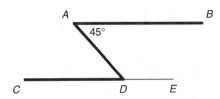

The types of angles formed are alternate interior angles.

Step 3.   If alternate interior angles are congruent, then the lines are parallel. Therefore, in order for $\overline{AB}$ to be parallel to $\overline{CE}$, the measure of $\angle ADC$ must be 45°.

The **slope** of a line is a measure of the "steepness" of a line. Two non-vertical lines are parallel when they have the same slope. Let's review the formula for slope:

$$\text{slope} = \frac{y_2 - y_1}{x_2 - x_1} \text{ or } \frac{\text{rise}}{\text{run}}$$

Example: Find the slope of the line containing the points $A(2, 5)$ and $B(6, {}^-3)$.

Solution 1: Use the formula. Let $A(2, 5) = (x_1, y_1)$ and $B(6, {}^-3) = (x_2, y_2)$.

$$\text{slope of } \overleftrightarrow{AB} = \frac{{}^-3 - 5}{6 - 2} = \frac{{}^-8}{4} = \frac{{}^-2}{1} = {}^-2$$

Solution 2: In a coordinate plane, the slope of $\overleftrightarrow{AB} = \frac{\text{rise}}{\text{run}}$.

REMEMBER

When moving in a coordinate plane to the left (run) or down (rise) the rise or run will be negative. Also, when moving to the right (run) or up (rise) the rise or run will be positive.

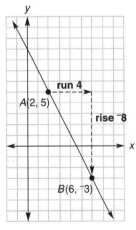

$$\text{slope of } \overleftrightarrow{AB} = \frac{\text{rise}}{\text{run}} = \frac{{}^-8}{4} = {}^-2$$

Model Problem 4   **Given:** $A(3, 4)$, $B(0, 8)$, $C(^-4, 5)$, and $D(^-7, 9)$.
Prove $\overleftrightarrow{AB} \parallel \overleftrightarrow{CD}$.

Solution   Find the slopes of $\overleftrightarrow{AB}$ and $\overleftrightarrow{CD}$.

$$\text{slope of } \overleftrightarrow{AB} = \frac{8-4}{0-3} = \frac{4}{-3}$$

$$\text{slope of } \overleftrightarrow{CD} = \frac{9-5}{^-7-(^-4)} = \frac{4}{-3}$$

The slopes are equal. Therefore, the lines are parallel.

Model Problem 5   **Given:** $A(^-4, 1)$, $B(1, 7)$, and $C(6, 3)$.
Find a point D in the first quadrant that will make $\overleftrightarrow{AB} \parallel \overleftrightarrow{CD}$.

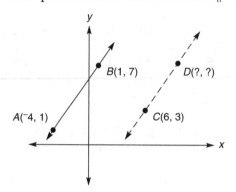

Solution   Step 1.   Find the slope of $\overleftrightarrow{AB}$. The slope of $\overleftrightarrow{AB} = \frac{\text{rise}}{\text{run}} = \frac{6}{5}$.

Step 2.   Use point C to locate a new point D that has a rise of 6 units and a run of 5 units from point C.

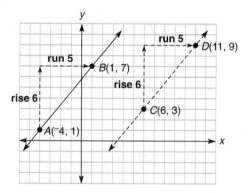

A point that has a rise of 6 units and a run of 5 units from point C is $D(11, 9)$. Therefore, the lines will be parallel if D is located at $(11, 9)$.

1. Which postulate or theorem justifies $a \parallel b$?

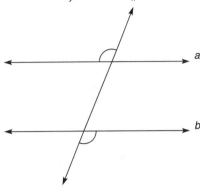

2. Which postulate or theorem justifies $a \parallel b$?

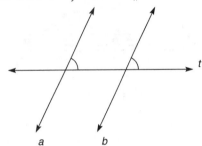

3. Line m will be parallel to line p when the value of x is _?_ .

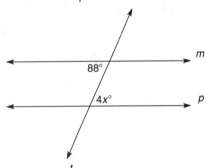

4. Name a pair of parallel lines in the figure below.

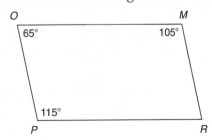

5. State whether $\overleftrightarrow{CD}$ is parallel to $\overleftrightarrow{XY}$ if $C(5, 10)$, $D(4, 6)$, $X(^-1, 4)$ and $Y(^-1, 12)$.

6. Find a point Y in the 2nd quadrant that will make $\overleftrightarrow{WZ} \parallel \overleftrightarrow{XY}$.

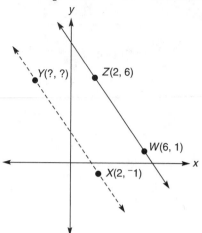

ASSESSMENT

1. Which postulate or theorem justifies $\overrightarrow{DC} \parallel \overrightarrow{EF}$?

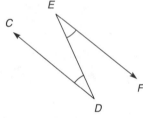

A If two lines are cut by a transversal and corresponding angles are congruent, then the lines are parallel.

B If two lines are cut by a transversal and vertical angles are congruent, then the lines are parallel.

C If two lines are cut by a transversal and alternate interior angles are supplementary, then the lines are parallel.

D If two lines are cut by a transversal and alternate interior angles are congruent, then the lines are parallel.

2. If $m\angle PQR = 120°$, which pair of lines are parallel?

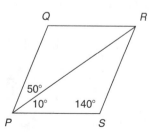

Hint: First find the measure of $\angle QPS$.

F $\overline{PQ} \parallel \overline{RS}$

G $\overline{PS} \parallel \overline{QR}$

H $\overline{PQ} \parallel \overline{PS}$

J $\overline{QR} \parallel \overline{RS}$

3.

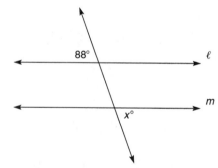

Line ℓ will be parallel to the line m when the value of x is ___.

A 92°

B 102°

C 88°

D 44°

4. If the slope of $\overleftrightarrow{WY}$ is $\frac{-3}{4}$, which represents the slope of $\overleftrightarrow{XZ}$ that makes $\overleftrightarrow{XZ}$ parallel to $\overleftrightarrow{WY}$?

F $\frac{-3}{4}$

G $\frac{-4}{3}$

H $\frac{3}{4}$

J $\frac{4}{3}$

5. Find the value of x that makes line m parallel to line n.

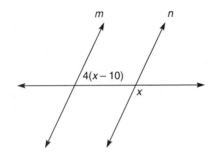

A 3.33

B 13.33

C 38

D 44

6. Which coordinates for F will make $\overline{FG} \parallel \overline{HJ}$?

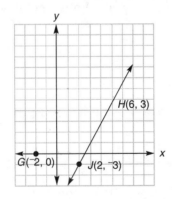

F $(0, 3)$

G $(3, 0)$

H $(3, {}^-1)$

J $(1, 2)$

7. Which pair of lines are parallel?

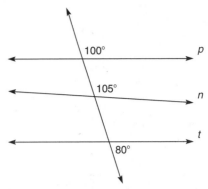

A $p \parallel n$

B $n \parallel t$

C $n \parallel p$

D $p \parallel t$

8. Find the value of x that makes $j \parallel p$.

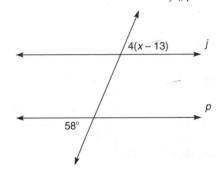

F 27.5

G 33.75

H 43.5

J 58

9. Use only the marked angles.

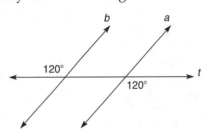

Why is line a parallel to line b?

A Alternate exterior angles are congruent, so the lines are parallel.

B Alternate exterior angles are supplementary, so the lines are parallel.

C Corresponding angles are congruent, so the lines are parallel.

D Corresponding angles are supplementary, so the lines are parallel.

10. **Given:** $D(3, 0)$, $C(^-2, 4)$, and $W(6, 0)$.

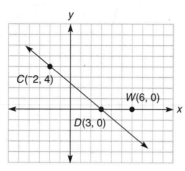

Which coordinates for X will make $\overleftrightarrow{CD} \parallel \overleftrightarrow{WX}$?

F $(5, ^-2)$

G $(1, 4)$

H $(2, ^-5)$

J $(^-4, 1)$

11. The measure of $\angle EFA$ is 40° and the measure of $\angle DEF$ is 80°.

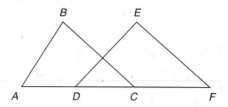

Which of the following angles must also measure 40° in order for $\overline{BC}$ to be parallel to $\overline{EF}$?

A $\angle BAF$

B $\angle EDF$

C $\angle BCA$

D $\angle BCF$

PRACTICE 4 Constructions with Compass and Straightedge— Working with Angles

Objective:	SOL G.11

☐ The student will construct a line segment congruent to a given line segment, the bisector of a line segment, a perpendicular to a given line from a point not on the line, a perpendicular to a given line at a point on the line, the bisector of a given angle, and an angle congruent to a given angle.

REMEMBER

If you are given a ruler to use as a straightedge, please remember not to use it to measure lengths.

Construction problems that appear on the test can be constructed by using a single instrument, a sheet of patty paper, or a combination of two instruments, a straightedge and a compass.

Note: A sheet of patty paper is simply a square piece of transparent waxed paper.

There are many types of constructions in geometry, but you need to be concerned with only six basic constructions. The model problems will give a review of the procedures used in each of the six constructions listed in the objective.

Model Problem 1 Given: $\overline{CD}$.

Construct a line segment $\overline{AX}$ congruent to line segment $\overline{CD}$.

Straightedge and Compass:

Step 1. Use your straightedge to draw a line on your paper. Choose any point on that line and label it point *A*.

Step 2. Adjust your compass to correspond to the length of $\overline{CD}$.

Step 3. Without changing the compass setting, place the tip of your compass on point *A* and draw an arc that intersects the line. Label the intersection *X*.

Result: Since we adjusted our compass to the length of $\overline{CD}$, $\overline{AX} \cong \overline{CD}$.

Patty Paper:

Step 1. Place a piece of patty paper on top of the given segment. Trace the given segment and its end points.

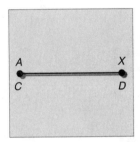

REMEMBER

For the patty paper constructions, use the straightedge to help you draw straight lines.

Step 2. Slide the piece of patty paper down in order to see the given segment.

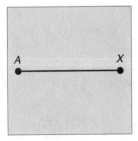

Result: The given segment and the tracing on the patty paper are congruent.

Model Problem 2   Given: $\overline{AB}$.

Construct the bisector of $\overline{AB}$.

> **Note:** A **bisector** of a line segment is any line dividing the given segment into two equal parts. The **perpendicular bisector** is the bisector that is also perpendicular to the given line segment.

Straightedge and Compass:

Step 1. Place your compass on point A and adjust the compass to more than half the length of $\overline{AB}$. With this compass setting, draw an arc above and below $\overline{AB}$.

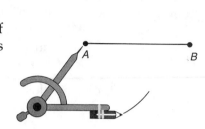

Step 2. Without changing the compass setting, place the tip of the compass on point B. Draw an arc above and below $\overline{AB}$ intersecting the two previously drawn arcs. Label the intersections X and Y.

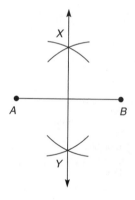

Step 3. Use your straightedge to draw a line through X and Y.

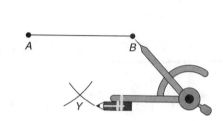

Result: $\overleftrightarrow{XY}$ bisects $\overline{AB}$.

Patty Paper:

Step 1. Copy the line segment on a piece of patty paper like you did in Model Problem 1.

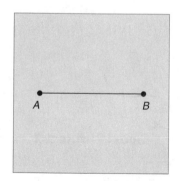

Step 2. Fold the patty paper so that the endpoints lie on top of each other. Then crease the patty paper after lining up the endpoints.

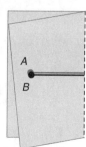

Step 3. Open the paper.

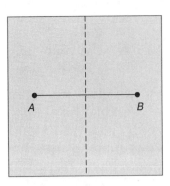

Result: The crease is the bisector of $\overline{AB}$ since it divides the line segment into two equal parts.

Note: Line $\overleftrightarrow{XY}$ and the creased line are both perpendicular to $\overline{AB}$. Thus, the above two constructions result in the perpendicular bisector of the given line segment.

Model Problem 3   **Given:** Point X not on line t.
Construct a line perpendicular to line t passing through X.

Straightedge and Compass:

Step 1.   With X as the center, draw an arc that intersects line t at two points. Label these points A and B.

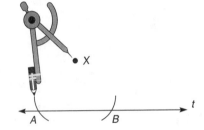

Step 2.   Open the compass to more than half the length of $\overleftrightarrow{AB}$. With A as the center, draw an arc below line t.

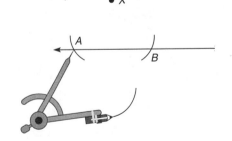

Step 3.   With the same compass setting, place the tip of the compass on B and draw an arc below line t. Label the intersection Y.

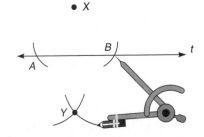

Step 4. Use your straightedge to draw a line through X and Y.

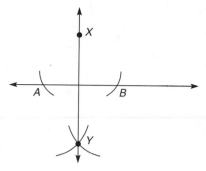

Result: $\overleftrightarrow{XY}$ is perpendicular to line t and passes through the point X.

Note: If X is below the line segment, simply turn the figure over and follow the same instructions as before, starting from Step 1.

Patty Paper: **Step 1.** Copy the given sketch on a piece of patty paper.

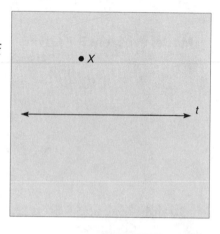

Step 2. Fold the line t on top of itself until the folded edge passes through the point X. Crease the paper.

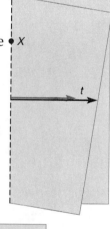

Step 3. Unfold and flatten.

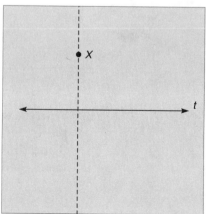

Result: The crease is the line perpendicular to line *t* passing through the point X.

Model Problem 4   **Given:** Point *A* on line *l*.
Construct a line perpendicular to line *l* passing through *A*.

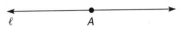

Straightedge and Compass: Step 1.   With *A* as the center, draw an arc that intersects line *l* at two points. Label these points *X* and *Y*.

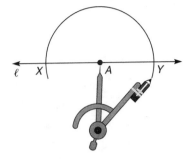

Step 2.   Open the compass to more than half the length of $\overline{XY}$. Draw two arcs from points *X* and *Y* above line *l*. Label the intersection *Z*.

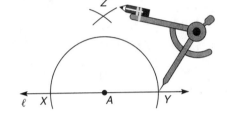

Step 3.   Use your straightedge to draw a line through *A* and *Z*.

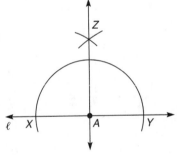

Result: $\overleftrightarrow{ZA}$ is perpendicular to line *l* and passes through the point *A*.

Patty Paper: Step 1.   Copy the given sketch on a piece of patty paper.

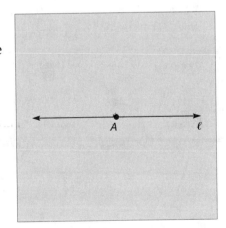

Step 2. Fold the line ℓ on top of itself until the folded edge passes through the point A.

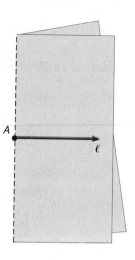

Step 3. Unfold and flatten.

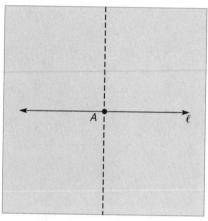

Result: The crease is the line perpendicular to line ℓ passing through the point A.

Model Problem 5 Given: $\angle BAC$.

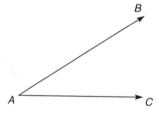

Construct the angle bisector of $\angle BAC$.

Note: An **angle bisector** is a ray dividing an angle into two equal parts.

Straightedge and Compass: Step 1. Open the compass to a convenient radius. With A as the center, draw two arcs that intersect the sides of $\angle BAC$. Label the intersections X and Y.

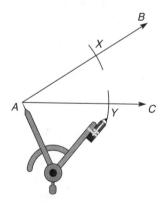

Step 2. Adjust the compass to more than half the length of $\overline{XY}$. With X as the center, draw an arc inside of $\angle BAC$. With the same compass setting, place the tip of the compass on Y. Draw an arc inside of $\angle BAC$ intersecting the first arc. Label the intersection Z.

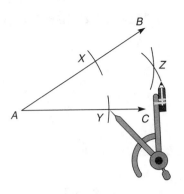

Step 3. With your straightedge, draw $\overrightarrow{AZ}$.

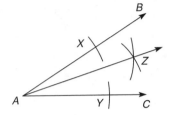

Result: $\overrightarrow{AZ}$ is the angle bisector of $\angle BAC$.

Patty Paper: Step 1. Copy the given figure on a piece of patty paper.

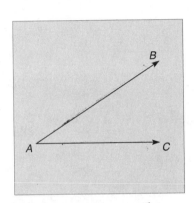

Step 2. Fold $\overrightarrow{AB}$ on top of $\overrightarrow{AC}$ until the folded edge passes through the point A. Crease the paper.

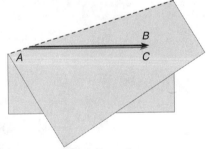

Step 3. Open the patty paper and inspect the angle.

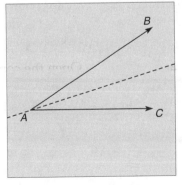

Result: The crease is the angle bisector of $\angle BAC$ since it divides the given angle into two equal parts.

Model Problem 6   Given: $\angle X$.

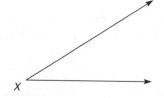

Construct an angle congruent to $\angle X$.

Straightedge and Compass:

Step 1.   Draw a ray and label it $\overrightarrow{AB}$.

Step 2.   Open the compass to a convenient radius. With X as the center, draw an arc intersecting the sides of $\angle X$. Label the intersections Y and Z.

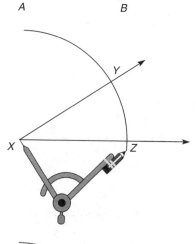

Step 3.   With the same compass settings from Step 2, use A as the center to draw an arc that is the same size as the arc from Step 2. Label C the intersection of the arc and $\overrightarrow{AB}$.

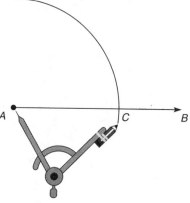

Step 4.   Adjust your compass to correspond to the distance between Y and Z. With this setting, place the tip of the compass on C and draw an arc that intersects the arc drawn in the previous step. Label the intersection D.

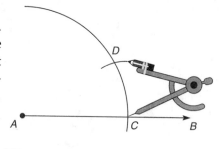

Step 5.   With your straightedge, draw $\overrightarrow{AD}$.

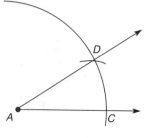

Result: $\angle DAC$ is congruent to $\angle X$.

Patty Paper: Step 1. Copy the given figure on a piece of patty paper.

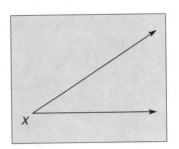

Step 2. Slide the piece of patty paper down in order to see the given angle.

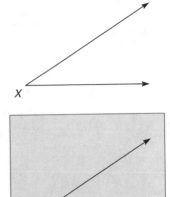

Result: The given angle and the tracing on the patty paper are congruent.

TRY THESE

For problems 1–5, use only a straightedge and a compass.

1. Construct $\overline{WX}$ so that $\overline{WX} \cong \overline{CD}$.

2. Construct a line perpendicular to line *t* through point *P*.

3. Construct the perpendicular bisector of $\overline{LM}$.

4. Construct a line perpendicular to $\overline{BD}$ through point A.

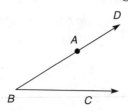

5. Construct $\angle QRS$ congruent to $\angle MNO$.

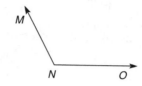

For problems 6 and 7, use the patty paper constructions.

6. Bisect $\angle BOX$.

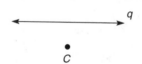

7. Construct a line perpendicular to line q from point C.

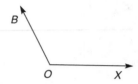

 ASSESSMENT

Use either patty paper or a straightedge and a compass for the problems in this section.

1. Which shows a line segment bisector?

A

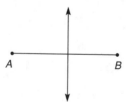

C

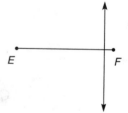

B

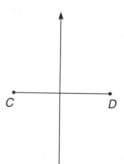

D

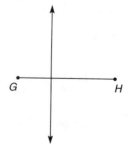

2. Construct a line perpendicular to $\overleftrightarrow{OP}$ passing through the point X. What other point does it pass through?

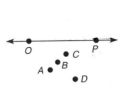

F A

G B

H C

J D

3. If a line were constructed perpendicular to $\overrightarrow{BA}$ at point A, which other point would it pass through?

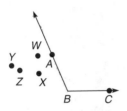

A W

B X

C Y

D Z

4. Which construction represents an angle bisector?

F

G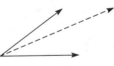

H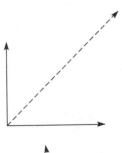

J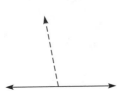

5. Which segment is congruent to the given segment $\overline{ZW}$?

A $\overline{KM}$

B $\overline{KL}$

C $\overline{LO}$

D $\overline{NO}$

6. Which angle is congruent to $\angle RST$?

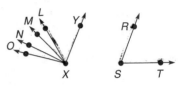

F $\angle LXY$

G $\angle MXY$

H $\angle NXY$

J $\angle OXY$

7. Which represents the construction of a segment whose length is $a + b$?

A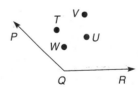

B

C

D

8. The angle bisector of $\angle PQR$ goes through which point?

F T

G U

H V

J W

9. Construct a line perpendicular to $\overline{AC}$ at point B. What other point does it pass through?

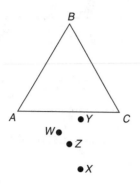

A W

B X

C Y

D Z

10. Construct the perpendicular bisector of $\overline{MN}$. Find the point that lies on the perpendicular bisector of $\overline{MN}$.

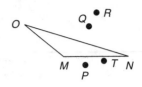

F Q

G P

H R

J T

PRACTICE 5   Cumulative Practice on SOLs G.3, 4, and 11

1. Given the figure below, what is the measure of $\angle 1$?

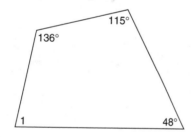

A $42°$

B $48°$

C $61°$

D $132°$

2. **Given:** $m\angle 1 = (4x - 10)$ and $m\angle 2 = (2x - 14)$.

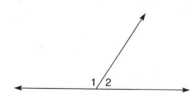

Find the value of x.

F 64

G 34

H 19

J 8

3. In which figure is line n parallel to line m?

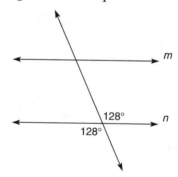

C

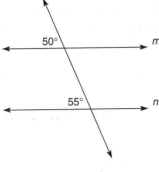

D

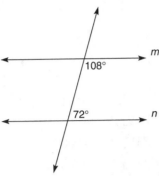

4. Given the figure below, find the value of x.

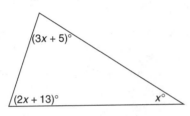

    F 27°

    G 30°

    H 32.66°

    J 39.2°

5. Two supplementary angles are in the ratio of 13:5. Find the measures of the two angles.

    A 65° and 25°

    B 130° and 50°

    C 143° and 55°

    D 260° and 100°

6. **Given:** ∠*ABC* is a right angle, m∠*ABE* = m∠*DBC*, and m∠*EBD* = 20°.

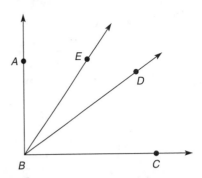

Find m∠*ABE*.

    F 80°

    G 45°

    H 35°

    J 20°

7. Given the figure below, find the measure of ∠*TOU*.

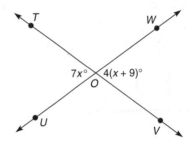

    A 13°

    B 15°

    C 21°

    D 84°

8. **Given:** ∠*ABE* is a right angle, m∠3 = (2x + 5), m∠4 = 3x.

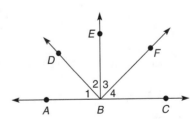

What is m∠3?

    F 17°

    G 39°

    H 45°

    J 51°

9. **Given:** $p \parallel q$.

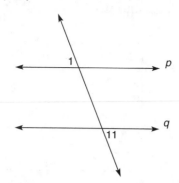

Why is $\angle 1$ congruent to $\angle 11$?

A If two parallel lines are cut by a transversal, then alternate exterior angles are congruent.

B If two parallel lines are cut by a transversal, then consecutive interior angles are congruent.

C If two parallel lines are cut by a transversal, then corresponding angles are congruent.

D If two parallel lines are cut by a transversal, then vertical angles are congruent.

10.

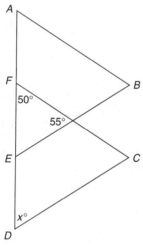

$\overline{EB}$ is parallel to $\overline{DC}$ when the value of x is ___?___.

F 50°

G 55°

H 75°

J 95°

11. $\overrightarrow{WY}$ will be parallel to $\overrightarrow{XP}$ when which of the following is true?

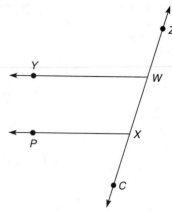

A $\angle YWX \cong \angle PXW$

B $\angle ZWY \cong \angle PXC$

C $\angle ZWY \cong \angle WXP$

D $\angle ZWY \cong \angle YWX$

12. **Given:** $q \parallel p$, m$\angle 5 = (x + 50)$, and m$\angle 6 = 3x$.

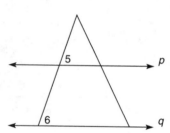

Find the measure of $\angle 5$.

F 10°

G 25°

H 50°

J 75°

13. What is the measure of $\angle XYZ$?

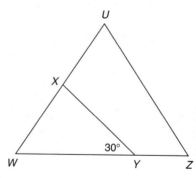

A 60°

B 90°

C 100°

D 150°

14. Given: $\angle 2$ is complementary to $\angle 3$, and $m\angle 1 = 151°$.

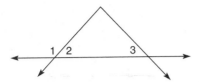

Find the measure of $\angle 3$.

F 151°

G 61°

H 45°

J 29°

15. Which point lies on the angle bisector of $\angle GHI$?

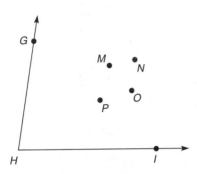

A M

B N

C O

D P

16. When a beam of light is reflected off a mirror, it forms an angle of incidence that is congruent to the angle of reflection.

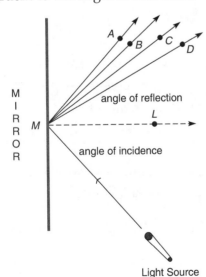

Which angle represents the angle of reflection?

F $\angle AML$

G $\angle BML$

H $\angle CML$

J $\angle DML$

17. Construct the line perpendicular to line t passing through P. Which other point does the line pass through?

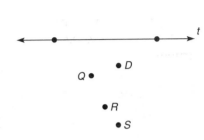

A D

B Q

C R

D S

18. Given the figure below, find the value of x.

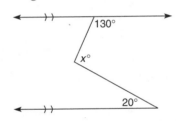

F 20°

G 50°

H 70°

J 75°

19. Given: $\square ABCD$.

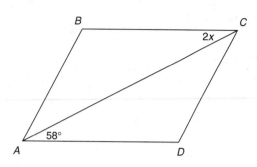

Find the value of x.

A 16

B 29

C 32

D 58

20. In which figure is line n *not* parallel to line m?

F

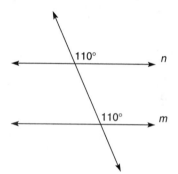

G

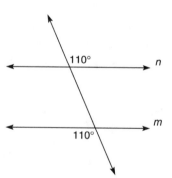

H

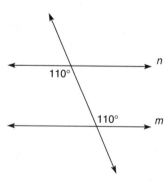

J

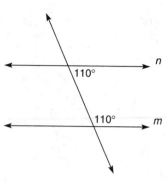

21. Given the figure below, find the value of x.

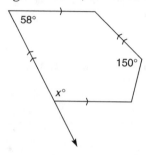

A 122°

B 58°

C 30°

D 22°

22. Which coordinates for P make $\overline{XY} \parallel \overline{WP}$?

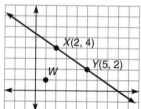

F (7, ⁻5)

G (4, 4)

H (1, 4)

J (⁻2, 3)

23. Given: $A(⁻5, 5)$, $B(⁻3, 3)$, $C(7, 8)$ and $D(7, 11)$. Which statement is true?

A $\overline{AB}$ is parallel to $\overline{AC}$.

B $\overline{AB}$ is parallel to $\overline{CD}$.

C $\overline{AC}$ is parallel to $\overline{BD}$.

D $\overline{AD}$ is parallel to $\overline{BC}$.

24. What is the measure of $\angle 4$?

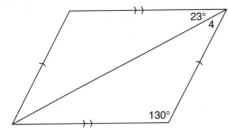

F 130°

G 50°

H 27°

J 23°

25. Given the figure below, what is the value of x that makes line a parallel to line b?

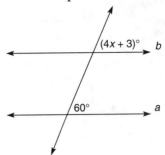

A $\dfrac{27}{4}$

B $\dfrac{57}{4}$

C $\dfrac{63}{4}$

D $\dfrac{117}{4}$

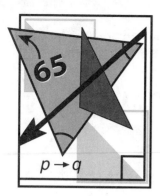

UNIT 2
Triangles and Logic

PRACTICE 6   Identifying the Converse, Inverse, and Contrapositive of a Conditional Statement

☐ The student will construct and judge the validity of a logical argument consisting of a set of premises and a conclusion. This will include identifying the converse, inverse, and contrapositive of a conditional statement.

The Conditional   A **conditional statement**, also called an **if-then statement**, consists of two parts; the **hypothesis** (or **antecedent**), which is usually located after the word *if*, and the **conclusion** (or **consequent**), which is located after the word *then*.

> **Example**   If $\underbrace{\text{it is raining}}_{\text{hypothesis}}$, then $\underbrace{\text{the sky is cloudy}}_{\text{conclusion}}$.

Note: A hypothesis and a conclusion must be sentences or parts of sentences that can be judged to be either true or false. For example, "Where is the post office?" cannot be a hypothesis or a conclusion since it has no truth value.

Hidden Conditionals   Often the words *if . . . then . . .* do not appear in a sentence. This type of sentence is called a **hidden conditional**. In such cases, you need to rewrite the words in the sentence so that the conditional form *if . . . then . . .* becomes more obvious.

Examples

1. "A resident of Richmond is a resident of Virginia" becomes "*If* you reside in Richmond, *then* you reside in Virginia."
2. "Corresponding angles are congruent when formed by a transversal cutting two parallel lines" becomes "*If* a transversal cuts two parallel lines, *then* the corresponding angles formed are congruent."
3. "She loves math if she's a math teacher" becomes "*If* she's a math teacher, *then* she loves math."
4. "The two angles are vertical angles; thus, the two angles are congruent" becomes "*If* two angles are vertical angles, *then* the two angles are congruent."

The Converse, Inverse, and Contrapositive of a Conditional

When you interchange the hypothesis and the conclusion of a conditional, you get a new statement called the **converse** of the original statement.

Example

Conditional: If it is raining, then the sky is cloudy.
              <u>hypothesis</u>   <u>conclusion</u>

Converse: If the sky is cloudy, then it is raining.
           <u>conclusion</u>   <u>hypothesis</u>

In addition to the converse, there are two other statements that can be formed from a conditional. These are given in the table below:

STATEMENT	FORM IN WORDS
Conditional	If the <u>hypothesis</u>, then the **conclusion**.
Converse	If the **conclusion**, then the <u>hypothesis</u>.
Inverse	If *not* the <u>hypothesis</u>, then *not* the **conclusion**.
Contrapositive	If *not* the **conclusion**, then *not* the <u>hypothesis</u>.

REMEMBER
The negation of the hypothesis and the negation of the conclusion form the inverse statement, and taking the converse of the inverse forms the contrapositive statement.

Model Problem 1 Write the converse of the statement, "If a triangle is equilateral, then the sides are congruent."

Solution Conditional: If a triangle is equilateral, then the sides are congruent.
                           <u>hypothesis</u>   <u>conclusion</u>

Converse: If the sides are congruent, then the triangle is equilateral.
           <u>conclusion</u>   <u>hypothesis</u>

Model Problem 2 Write the inverse of the statement, "If it snows, then I will wear my boots."

Solution Conditional: If it snows, then I will wear my boots.
                           <u>hypothesis</u>   <u>conclusion</u>

Inverse: If it does not snow, then I will not wear my boots.
          <u>not the hypothesis</u>   <u>not the conclusion</u>

Model Problem 3 Write the contrapositive of the statement, "If it is raining, then the sidewalk is wet."

Solution Conditional: If it is raining, then the sidewalk is wet.
                           <u>hypothesis</u>   <u>conclusion</u>

Contrapositive: If the sidewalk is not wet, then it is not raining.
                 <u>not the conclusion</u>   <u>not the hypothesis</u>

Model Problem 4 Write the contrapositive of the statement, "A quadrilateral that is a rectangle is a parallelogram."

Solution Rewrite the hidden conditional.

Conditional: If a quadrilateral is a rectangle, then it is a parallelogram.

Contrapositive: If a quadrilateral is not a parallelogram, then it is not a rectangle.

> **Note:** A conditional and its contrapositive are **logically equivalent** or "say the same thing." Thus, a conditional and its contrapositive *always* have the same truth values. However, the same is not true of converses and inverses: a conditional can be true, but its converse and inverse can both be false.

Model Problem 5 Given the statement, "If two angles are right angles, then they are congruent," write its converse and determine the truth value of the converse.

Solution Converse: If two angles are congruent, then they are right angles.

The converse is false because not all congruent angles are right angles.

Model Problem 6 Write a sentence that is logically equivalent to the statement, "If two lines are perpendicular, then the four angles formed are congruent."

Solution A conditional and its contrapositive are logically equivalent.

Contrapositive: If the four angles formed by two intersecting lines are not congruent, then the two lines are not perpendicular.

The Biconditional When you replace the words *if . . . then . . .* in a conditional by the words *if and only if*, you get a new statement called the **biconditional**.

Example If ∠ABC is a right angle, then m∠ABC = 90°.
∠ABC is a right angle if and only if m∠ABC = 90°.

> **Note:** A biconditional statement is true *only* when the conditional and its converse have the same truth values.

 TRY THESE

1. For each statement, write the converse.
    "If a flower is a rose, then it has thorns."
    "If △ABC is equilateral, then it has three congruent sides."

2. For each statement, write the contrapositive.
    "If tomorrow is Tuesday, then yesterday was Sunday."
    "If I am in Virginia, then I am in the United States."

3. For each statement, write the inverse.

   "If two lines are parallel, then alternate interior angles are congruent."

   "If a polygon is a pentagon, then the sum of the interior angles is 540°."

4. Write the inverse of the statement, "If $a = b$, then $a^2 = b^2$," and determine the truth value of the inverse.

5. Given the sentence, "If two lines are cut by a transversal and consecutive interior angles are supplementary, then the two lines are parallel," determine the truth value of its contrapositive.

6. For each statement, write the converse and biconditional, and determine the truth value of the converse and biconditional.

   "If two angles are vertical angles, then the angles are congruent."

   "If two angles form a linear pair, then the angles are supplementary."

 ASSESSMENT

1. Which is the inverse of the statement, "If Jill lives in Richmond, then she lives in Virginia"?

   A If Jill lives in Virginia, then she lives in Richmond.

   B If Jill lives in Virginia, then she does not live in Richmond.

   C If Jill does not live in Virginia, then she does not live in Richmond.

   D If Jill does not live in Richmond, then she does not live in Virginia.

2. Which is the converse of the statement, "If you're at least 18 years old, then you can vote"?

   F If you can vote, then you're at least 18 years old.

   G If you're not at least 18 years old, then you can't vote.

   H If you're at least 18 years old, then you can't vote.

   J If you can vote, then you're not at least 18 years old.

3 Which is the converse of the statement, "If the sidewalk is wet, then it is raining"?

   A If it is raining, then the sidewalk is wet.

   B If it is not raining, then the sidewalk is not wet.

   C If the sidewalk is wet, then it is not raining.

   D If the sidewalk is not wet, then it is raining.

4. Which is the inverse of the statement, "If the sky is not cloudy, then it is not raining"?

   F If it is not raining, then the sky is not cloudy.

   G If the sky is cloudy, then it is raining.

   H If it is raining, then the sky is cloudy.

   J If it is not raining, then the sky is cloudy.

5. Which is the contrapositive of the statement, "If $2x + 5 = 13$, then $x = 4$"?

   A If $x \neq 4$, then $2x + 5 \neq 13$.

   B If $2x + 5 \neq 13$, then $x \neq 4$.

   C If $x = 4$, then $2x + 5 = 13$.

   D If $2x + 5 \neq 13$, then $x = 4$.

6. Which is the converse of the statement, "If good food is served, then the dinner party is successful"?

   F If good food is not served, then the dinner party is not successful.

   G If the dinner party is not successful, then good food is not served.

   H If good food is served, then the dinner party is not successful.

   J If the dinner party is successful, then good food is served.

7. Which is the contrapositive of the statement, "If two angles are supplementary, then the sum of the two angles is 180°"?

   A If the sum of two angles is 180°, then the two angles are supplementary.

   B If two angles are not supplementary, then the sum of the two angles is not 180°.

   C If the sum of two angles is not 180°, then the two angles are not supplementary.

   D If two angles are not supplementary, then the sum of the two angles is less than 180°.

8. Which is the inverse of the statement, "If Sharon can go, then Ruth cannot go"?

   F If Sharon cannot go, then Ruth can go.

   G If Ruth cannot go, then Sharon can go.

   H If Ruth can go, then Sharon cannot go.

   J If Sharon cannot go, then Ruth cannot go.

9. Which is the biconditional of the statement, "If two angles have the same measure, then they are congruent"?

   A Two angles do not have the same measure if and only if they are not congruent.

   B Two angles have the same measure if and only if they are congruent.

   C If two angles are congruent, then they have the same measure.

   D If two angles are not congruent, then they do not have the same measure.

PRACTICE 7   Translating Short Verbal Arguments Into Symbolic Form

Objective: **SOL G.1b**

☐ The student will construct and judge the validity of a logical argument consisting of a set of premises and a conclusion. This will include translating a short verbal argument into symbolic form.

Translating Sentences Into Symbolic Form

When translating a sentence from English into symbolic form, there are certain commonly used symbols that you will find helpful. They are located in the table:

REMEMBER

To show the negation of a statement, place the symbol ~ before the letter representing the original statement. For example, if *p* represents "Today is Monday," then ~*p* represents "Today is *not* Monday."

SYMBOL	REPRESENTS
$\Rightarrow$ or $\rightarrow$	If . . . then . . .
~	The not of (negation)
$\wedge$	And (conjunction)
$\vee$	Or (disjunction)
$\Leftrightarrow$	If and only if
$a, b, c, ...$	Hypotheses, conclusions, and other simple sentences.

Note: *p* is usually used to represent the hypothesis of a conditional; *q* is usually used to represent the conclusion.

Model Problem 1   Let *s* represent "It is September."

Let *o* represent "It is October."

Let *w* represent "My watch has stopped."

Write the following sentences in symbolic form.

a If it is September, then it is not October.

b If it is not October, then my watch has stopped.

c It is not September and my watch has not stopped.

Solution

STATEMENT IN WORDS	SYMBOL

a If it is September, then it is not October. $s \rightarrow \sim o$

                  s   not *o*

b If it is not October, then my watch has stopped. $\sim o \rightarrow w$

           not *o*   *w*

c It is not September, and my watch has not stopped. $\sim s \wedge \sim w$

           not *s* $\wedge$ not *w*

> **Note:** In a conjunction ($a \wedge b$) and a disjunction ($a \vee b$), the order of the symbols does not matter. For example, $\sim p \wedge \sim r$ is equivalent to $\sim r \wedge \sim p$.

Model Problem 2   Write the following sentences in symbolic form.

a $m\angle A = 90°$ and $m\angle A = m\angle B$.

b The inverse of "If $m\angle A = 90°$, then $\angle B$ is a right angle."

c The converse of "If $\angle B$ is not a right angle, then $m\angle A \neq m\angle B$."

Solution   Let *p* represent "$m\angle A = 90°$."

Let *q* represent "$m\angle A = m\angle B$."

Let *r* represent "$\angle B$ is a right angle."

STATEMENT IN WORDS	SYMBOL

a $m\angle A = 90°$ and $m\angle A = m\angle B$. $p \wedge q$

         p $\wedge$ *q*

b Inverse: If $m\angle A \neq 90°$, then $\angle B$ is not a right angle. $\sim p \rightarrow \sim r$

                 not *p*   not *r*

c Converse: If $m\angle A \neq m\angle B$, then $\angle B$ is not a right angle. $\sim q \rightarrow \sim r$

                 not *q*   not *r*

Model Problem 3   Let *c* represent "*x* is an even number."

Let *d* represent "*x* is a multiple of 5."

Suppose that *x* has the value of 50. Write a true sentence in symbolic form using conjunction ($\land$) and the given symbols.

Solution   When *x* has a value of 50, *c* and *d* become the following:

c: 50 is an even number.

d: 50 is a multiple of 5.

These are both true statements. Therefore, $c \land d$ or "50 is an even number *and* 50 is a multiple of 5" is also a true statement.

Translating Arguments Into Symbolic Form

A **logical argument** is a series of statements called **premises** or **hypotheses** followed by a final statement called the **conclusion**. We say that the conclusion logically follows the premises if, by the laws of reasoning, the premises force the conclusion to be true. An argument satisfying this condition is called a **valid argument**.

We will review arguments that use the law of detachment (modus ponens), the law of the contrapositive (modus tollens), and the law of syllogism (the chain rule).

ARGUMENT USES	SYMBOLIC FORM		EXAMPLE
The Law of Detachment	Premises:	$p \to q$	If it is raining, then the sidewalk is wet.
		p	It is raining.
	Conclusion:	q	Therefore, the sidewalk is wet.
The Law of the Contrapositive	Premises:	$p \to q$	If it is raining, then the sidewalk is wet.
		$\sim q$	The sidewalk is not wet.
	Conclusion:	$\sim p$	Therefore, it is not raining.
The Law of Syllogism	Premises:	$p \to q$	If it is raining, then the sidewalk is wet.
		$q \to r$	If the sidewalk is wet, then the grass is muddy.
	Conclusion:	$p \to r$	Therefore, if it is raining, then the grass is muddy.

Model Problem 4   Write the following argument in symbolic form and determine if it is an instance of the law of detachment, the contrapositive, or syllogism.

If you study hard, then you will earn a good grade on the test.

If you earn a good grade on the test, then your parents will be happy.

Therefore, if you study hard, then your parents will be happy.

Solution   Let *p* represent "You study hard."

Let *q* represent "You will earn a good grade on the test."

Let *r* represent "Your parents will be happy."

STATEMENT IN WORDS	SYMBOL
If you study hard, then you will earn a good grade on the test.	$p \rightarrow q$
If you earn a good grade on the test, then your parents will be happy.	$q \rightarrow r$
Therefore, if you study hard, then your parents will be happy.	$\therefore p \rightarrow r$

This is an example of the law of syllogism.

Model Problem 5   Write the following argument in symbolic form and determine if it is an instance of the law of detachment, the contrapositive, or syllogism.

> If a student plays baseball, then he/she must be passing all of his/her courses.
> Jim plays baseball.
> Therefore, Jim must be passing all of his courses.

Solution   Let p represent "A student plays baseball."

Let q represent "He/she must be passing all of his/her courses."

STATEMENT IN WORDS	SYMBOL
If a student plays baseball, then he/she must be passing all of his/her courses.	$p \rightarrow q$
Jim plays baseball.	p
Therefore, Jim must be passing all of his courses.	$\therefore q$

This is an example of the law of detachment (modus ponens).

TRY THESE

1. Let j represent "Jill stays home."
   Let t represent "Ted cannot go."
   Let i represent "I will go alone."
   Use the given symbols to write the following sentences in symbolic form.
   a   The inverse of "If Jill stays home, then I will go alone."
   b   The contrapositive of "If Ted can go, then I won't go alone."
   c   "Jill doesn't stay home and I won't go alone."

2. Write each sentence in English and in symbolic form.

 a The converse of "If a triangle has no congruent sides, then the triangle is scalene."

 b The biconditional of "If a triangle has no congruent sides, then the triangle is scalene."

 c The inverse of "If a triangle is scalene, then it is not equilateral."

3. Let d represent "x is an odd number."

 Let c represent "x is a prime number."

 Suppose that x has the value of 2. Use conjunction ($\land$) and the given symbols to write a true sentence.

4. Write each argument in symbolic form and determine if it is an instance of the law of detachment, the contrapositive, or syllogism.

 a If a creature is a mammal, then it is warm-blooded.

 Dogs are mammals.

 Therefore, dogs are warm-blooded.

 b If same-side interior angles are congruent, then the two lines are parallel.

 If two lines are parallel, then corresponding angles are congruent.

 Therefore, if same-side interior angles are congruent, then corresponding angles are congruent.

 c If a triangle is a right triangle, then it has a 90° angle.

 $\triangle ABC$ does not have a 90° angle.

 Therefore, $\triangle ABC$ is not a right triangle.

 ＡＳＳＥＳＳＭＥＮＴ

1. Let p represent "A figure is a cube."

 Let q represent "A figure has six lateral faces."

 Which of the following represents the sentence, "If a figure is not a cube, then it does not have six lateral faces"?

 A $\sim p \rightarrow \sim q$

 B $\sim q \rightarrow \sim p$

 C $q \rightarrow p$

 D $p \rightarrow q$

2. Let p represent "$x = 7$."

 Let q represent "$x + 3 = 10$."

 The symbolic form of the sentence, "If $x = 7$, then $x + 3 = 10$," is ? .

 F $p \lor q$

 G $p \land q$

 H $\sim p \rightarrow \sim q$

 J $p \rightarrow q$

3. Let n represent "A number is divisible by 4."

   Let d represent "It is divisible by 2."

   Which is the symbolic form of the statement, "If a number is not divisible by 4, then it is not divisible by 2"?

   A $n \rightarrow d$

   B $\sim n \rightarrow \sim d$

   C $\sim d \rightarrow n$

   D $d \rightarrow n$

4. Let p represent "The diagonals of a quadrilateral bisect each other."

   Let q represent "A quadrilateral is a parallelogram."

   Which is the symbolic form of the statement, "If a quadrilateral is not a parallelogram, then its diagonals do not bisect each other"?

   F $q \rightarrow p$

   G $\sim q \rightarrow \sim p$

   H $p \rightarrow q$

   J $\sim p \rightarrow \sim q$

5. Let p represent "Points that lie on the same line."

   Let q represent "They are collinear."

   Which is the symbolic form of the statement, "Points lie on the same line if and only if they are collinear"?

   A $p \Leftrightarrow q$

   B $\sim p \Leftrightarrow \sim q$

   C $p \rightarrow q$

   D $q \wedge p$

For problems 6–7, use the following symbols.
Let v represent "Two angles are vertical angles."
Let c represent "Two angles are congruent."
Let a represent "Two angles are adjacent."

6. Which is the symbolic form of the following argument?

   If two angles are vertical angles, then the two angles are congruent.

   $\angle A$ and $\angle B$ are vertical angles.

   Therefore, $\angle A$ and $\angle B$ are congruent.

   F $v \rightarrow a$
   v
   $\therefore a$

   G $v \rightarrow c$
   v
   $\therefore c$

   H $v \rightarrow c$
   c
   $\therefore v$

   J $v \rightarrow c$
   $\sim c$
   $\therefore \sim v$

7. Which is the symbolic form of the following argument?

   If two angles are vertical angles, then they are not adjacent.

   $\angle A$ and $\angle B$ are adjacent.

   Therefore, $\angle A$ and $\angle B$ are not vertical angles.

   A $v \rightarrow \sim a$
   a
   $\therefore \sim v$

   B $v \rightarrow \sim a$
   $\sim a$
   $\therefore \sim v$

   C $v \rightarrow \sim a$
   v
   $\therefore \sim a$

   D $v \rightarrow c$
   $c \rightarrow a$
   $\therefore v \rightarrow a$

8. The argument in the previous problem uses __?__.

   F modus ponens

   G the law of detachment

   H the law of the contrapositive

   J the law of syllogism

PRACTICE 8   Constructing and Validating Logical Arguments

Objective:	SOL G.1c & d

❐ The student will construct and judge the validity of a logical argument consisting of a set of premises and a conclusion. This will include using Venn diagrams to represent set relationships, and using deductive reasoning, including the law of syllogism.

Deductive reasoning is a process of reasoning from known facts or accepted principles to develop a new conclusion. Such reasoning is characterized as reasoning from the general to the particular. To arrive at a conclusion from a set of premises, first match the symbolic form of the premises to the general form of the three different types of arguments given in Practice 7 (Law of Detachment, Contrapositive, or Syllogism). Then, convert the symbolic form of the conclusion to its English equivalent.

Model Problem 1   Write a conclusion for each pair of true statements.

  a "If a polygon is regular, then it is equiangular."
  "If a polygon is equiangular, then its interior angles are congruent."

  b "If a creature is a dog, then it can bark."
  "Spike is a dog."

Solution

SYMBOL	STATEMENTS	REASONS
a $p \rightarrow q$	If a polygon is regular, then it is equiangular.	Premise
$q \rightarrow r$	If a polygon is equiangular, then its interior angles are congruent.	Premise
$\therefore p \rightarrow r$	Therefore, if a polygon is regular, then its interior angles are congruent.	Law of the Contrapositive
b $p \rightarrow q$	If a creature is a dog, then it can bark.	Premise
p	Spike is a dog.	Premise
$\therefore q$	Therefore, Spike can bark.	Law of Detachment

A useful tool for determining whether or not a conditional statement is true is a **Venn diagram**. These diagrams are helpful for visualizing logic statements containing negations.

STATEMENT	EXAMPLE	VENN DIAGRAM

Conditional: $p \rightarrow q$ If she goes, then I go.
Contrapositive: $\sim q \rightarrow \sim p$ If I won't go, then she won't go.

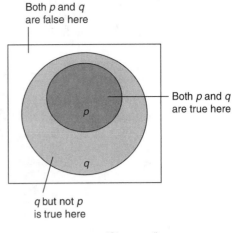

Both p and q are false here

Both p and q are true here

q but not p is true here

p = "She goes."
q = "I go."

Converse: $q \rightarrow p$ If I go, then she goes.
Inverse: $\sim p \rightarrow \sim q$ If she won't go, then I won't go.

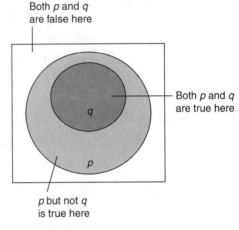

Both p and q are false here

Both p and q are true here

p but not q is true here

p = "She goes."
q = "I go."

Note: Since a conditional statement and its contrapositive are logically equivalent, they can be represented by the same Venn diagram. The converse and inverse of a statement are also logically equivalent. Thus, they are also represented by the same Venn diagram.

Model Problem 2   Explain each Venn diagram.

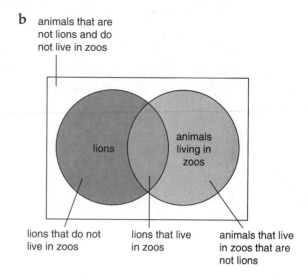

a   people who are not residents of Virginia

residents of Richmond

residents of Virginia

residents of Virginia who are not residents of Richmond

b   animals that are not lions and do not live in zoos

lions

animals living in zoos

lions that do not live in zoos

lions that live in zoos

animals that live in zoos that are not lions

Solution   **a**   The "residents of Richmond" circle is contained inside of the "residents of Virginia" circle. Therefore, the diagram tells us that all residents of Richmond are residents of Virginia.

b   The "lions" and "animals living in zoos" circles overlap. Therefore, the diagram tells us that some lions live in zoos (or some animals living in zoos are lions).

Model Problem 3   For each sentence, draw the corresponding Venn diagram.

a   If birds are singing, then it is not raining.

b   All vertical angles are congruent.

Solution   **a**

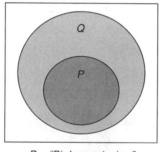

Q

P

P = "Birds are singing."
Q = "It is not raining."

b

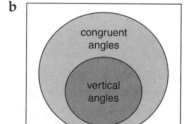

congruent angles

vertical angles

Model Problem 4

souvenir stores

clothing stores

Stores at Virginia Beach

The diagram shows that —

A   All stores at Virginia Beach sell either souvenirs or clothing.

B   All stores at Virginia Beach sell both souvenirs and clothing.

C No stores at Virginia Beach sell either souvenirs or clothing.

D Some stores at Virginia Beach sell both souvenirs and clothing.

Solution The "souvenir stores" and "clothing stores" circles overlap, indicating that there are stores that sell both souvenirs and clothing. Therefore, the correct answer is D.

Furthermore, the Venn diagram tells us that there are stores that sell only souvenirs, stores that sell only clothing, and stores that do not sell souvenirs or clothing.

Model Problem 5 Which of the following group of statements represents a valid argument?

A Given: $\begin{cases} \text{All triangles have three sides.} \\ \text{All equilateral triangles have three sides.} \end{cases}$
Conclusion: All triangles are equilateral.

B Given: $\begin{cases} \text{All polygons with congruent angles are equiangular.} \\ \text{All equilateral triangles have congruent angles.} \end{cases}$
Conclusion: All equilateral triangles are equiangular.

C Given: $\begin{cases} \text{All equiangular triangles have three sides.} \\ \text{All triangles have three sides.} \end{cases}$
Conclusion: All triangles are equiangular.

D Given: $\begin{cases} \text{All triangles are polygons.} \\ \text{All quadrilaterals are polygons.} \end{cases}$
Conclusion: All triangles are quadrilaterals.

Solution The answer is B. Draw a Venn diagram for the first premise.

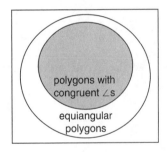

The second premise tells us to draw the "equilateral triangles" circle inside of the "polygons with congruent angles" circle.

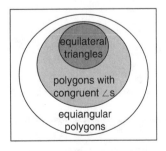

Since the "equilateral triangles" circle is also inside of the "equiangular polygons" circle, the Venn diagram tells us that any equilateral triangle is equiangular—which is exactly what the conclusion claims. Therefore, the Venn diagram for the premises contains the conclusion, and the argument is valid.

1. Write a conclusion for each pair of true statements.

   a "If $\triangle XYZ$ is isosceles, then it has two congruent sides."
   "$\triangle XYZ$ is isosceles."

   b "If a figure is a square, then all angles and sides are congruent."
   "If the angles and sides of a figure are all congruent, then it is a regular polygon."

   c "All squares are rectangles."
   "All rectangles are parallelograms."

   d "All lines with zero slope are horizontal."
   "Line l is not a horizontal line."

   e "If $\overline{DE}$ is the shortest side of $\triangle DEF$, then $\angle F$ is the smallest angle in $\triangle DEF$."
   "$\angle F$ is not the smallest angle in $\triangle DEF$."

2. Use the Venn diagram below to write a statement expressing the relationship between trapezoids and parallelograms.

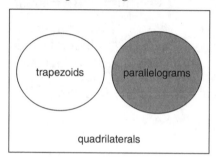

3. Write a conditional representing the Venn diagram below.

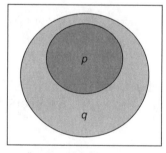

   p = "you are rich."
   q = "you can buy a Lamborghini."

4. Determine if each argument is valid.

   a Given: $\begin{cases} \text{All chimpanzees are bipeds.} \\ \text{All monkeys are bipeds.} \end{cases}$
   Conclusion: All monkeys are chimpanzees.

54 · Triangles and Logic

b Given: $\begin{cases} \text{If I have math, then I don't have biology.} \\ \text{If it's period 7, then I have math.} \end{cases}$
Conclusion: If it's period 7, then I don't have biology.

c Given: $\begin{cases} \text{All whales are mammals.} \\ \text{All mammals are warm-blooded.} \end{cases}$
Conclusion: All whales are warm-blooded.

 ＡＳＳＥＳＳＭＥＮＴ

1. Which conclusion logically follows the true statements?

   "If I add extra salt, then I will need a drink."

   "If I have popcorn at the movies, then I will add extra salt."

   A If I have popcorn at the movies, then I will not add extra salt.

   B If I do not add extra salt, then I will not need a drink.

   C If I have popcorn at the movies, then I will need a drink.

   D If I do not have popcorn at the movies, then I will not need a drink.

2. Which argument is valid?

   F Given: $\begin{cases} \text{All squares are parallelograms.} \\ \text{All rhombi are parallelograms.} \end{cases}$
   Conclusion: All rhombi are squares.

   G Given: $\begin{cases} \text{All squares are rhombi.} \\ \text{All rhombi are parallelograms.} \end{cases}$
   Conclusion: All squares are parallelograms.

   H Given: $\begin{cases} \text{All squares are parallelograms.} \\ \text{All rectangles are parallelograms.} \end{cases}$
   Conclusion: All rectangles are squares.

   J Given: $\begin{cases} \text{All squares are rectangles.} \\ \text{All rectangles are parallelograms.} \end{cases}$
   Conclusion: All parallelograms are rectangles.

3. The Venn diagram shows which statement?

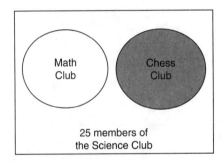

   A All 25 members of the Science Club belong to either the Chess Club or the Math Club.

   B All 25 members of the Science Club belong to both the Chess Club and the Math Club.

   C None of the 25 members of the Science Club belong to both the Chess Club and Math Club.

   D Some of the 25 members of the Science Club belong to both the Chess Club and the Math Club.

4. Which conclusion do the following statements justify?

"If x is positive, then $x^2 > 0$."

"If $x^2 > 0$, then $x > 0$."

F If x is not positive, then $x > 0$.

G $x^2 > 0$.

H x is positive.

J If x is positive, then $x > 0$.

5. Which diagram represents "All Datsuns are made in Japan"?

A

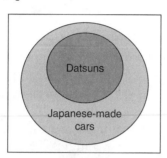

B

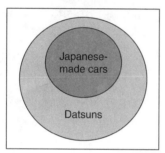

C

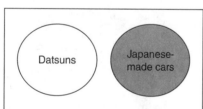

D

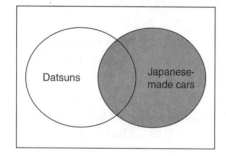

6. Which conclusion logically follows the true statements?

"If you live in Virginia Beach, then you live in Virginia."

"Beverly does not live in Virginia."

F Beverly lives in Virginia Beach.

G Beverly might live in Virginia Beach.

H Beverly does not live in Virginia Beach.

J Beverly might not live in Virginia Beach.

7.

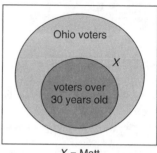

X = Matt

The given Venn diagram represents which of the following?

A Matt is a voter in Ohio, and he is over 30.

B Matt is a voter in Ohio, and he is not over 30.

C Matt is not a voter in Ohio, and he is over 30.

D Matt is not a voter in Ohio, and he is not over 30.

8. Which Venn diagram represents "Some collies make good pets"?

F

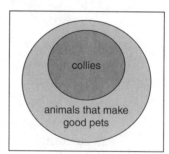

G

animals that make good pets / collies

H

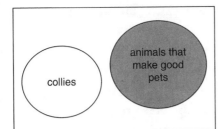

J

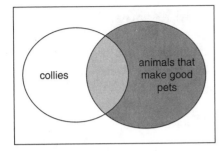

9. The Venn diagram shows which of the following?

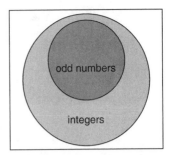

A If a number is not odd, then it is an integer.

B If a number is an integer, then it is odd.

C If a number is an integer, then it is not odd.

D If a number is odd, then it is an integer.

PRACTICE 9   Congruent and Similar Triangles

Objective: **SOL G.5a**

☐ **The student will investigate and identify congruence and similarity relationships between triangles.**

Congruent Triangles

Congruence and similarity are two geometric relationships that we will study in this practice. Two triangles are **congruent** when they have the same size and shape. This means that when two triangles are congruent, their vertices can be matched up so that corresponding parts of the triangles are congruent. For example, $\triangle ABC$ is congruent to $\triangle DEF$, denoted by $\triangle ABC \cong \triangle DEF$.

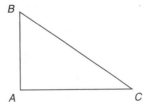

REMEMBER

When referring to congruent triangles, always name the corresponding vertices in the same order.

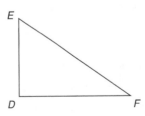

CORRESPONDING SIDES	CORRESPONDING ANGLES
$\overline{AB}$ and $\overline{DE}$	$\angle A$ and $\angle D$
$\overline{BC}$ and $\overline{EF}$	$\angle B$ and $\angle E$
$\overline{AC}$ and $\overline{DF}$	$\angle C$ and $\angle F$

Model Problem 1   Name the corresponding parts if △BIG ≅ △CAT in the figure below.

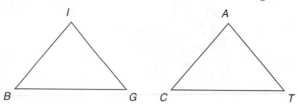

Solution   Corresponding angles: ∠B and ∠C; ∠I and ∠A; ∠G and ∠T.
Corresponding sides: $\overline{BI}$ and $\overline{CA}$; $\overline{IG}$ and $\overline{AT}$; $\overline{BG}$ and $\overline{CT}$.

Corresponding parts can be also identified with tick marks. Parts marked with the same number of tick marks are congruent.

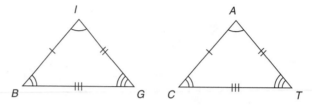

Model Problem 2   Use the diagram below to name two congruent triangles.

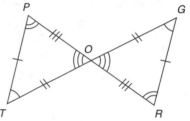

Solution   Reading the tick markings:
△TOP ≅ △GOR or △TPO ≅ △GRO or △OTP ≅ △OGR

Model Problem 3   The triangles below are congruent.

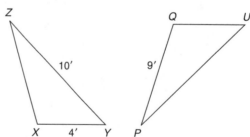

Complete the following.

a ∠Q ≅ ∠_?_
b ∠U ≅ ∠_?_
c ∠P ≅ ∠_?_
d ZX = _?_ ft.
e QU = _?_ ft.
f PU = _?_ ft.

Solution   Step 1.   Trace the first triangle (△XZY) with all markings and measures onto a sheet of patty paper.

Step 2. Match the patty paper drawing with the second triangle.

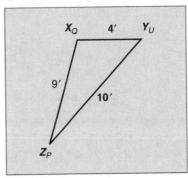

We see that $\triangle YXZ \cong \triangle UQP$.

Step 3. Now complete the answers for A–F.

    a $\angle Q \cong \angle X$

    b $\angle U \cong \angle Y$

    c $\angle P \cong \angle Z$

    d $ZX = 9$ ft.

    e $QU = 4$ ft.

    f $PU = 10$ ft.

Model Problem 4 Determine if $\triangle DEF \cong \triangle HIG$.

$\triangle DEF$: $D(2, 2)$, $E(6, 5)$, and $F(2, 5)$.

$\triangle HIG$: $H(^-7, 4)$, $I(^-3, 7)$, and $G(^-3, 4)$.

Solution Step 1. Graph the points on a sheet of graph paper and connect the points to form the two triangles.

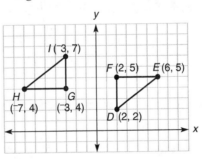

Step 2. Since congruent triangles have the same shape and size, it appears that the two triangles are congruent. We can verify that they are congruent by tracing one of the triangles on a sheet of patty paper and seeing if it matches up with the other triangle.

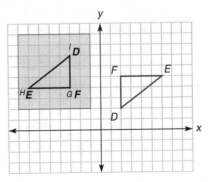

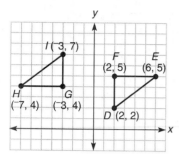

Or, we can count the number of units from one point to another to find the lengths of two sides of each triangle.

GI = 3 units	FD = 3 units
GH = 4 units	FE = 4 units

To find the lengths of the last two sides, use the Distance Formula, $\sqrt{(x_1 - x_2)^2 + y_1 - y_2)^2}$, where (x_1, y_1) is one point and (x_2, y_2) is the other point. To find the distance between points I and H, let $I(^-3, 7) = (x_1, y_1)$ and $H(^-7, 4) = (x_2, y_2)$.

$$IH = \sqrt{(^-3 - {}^-7)^2 + (7 - 4)^2} = \sqrt{(4)^2 + (3)^2}$$
$$IH = \sqrt{16 + 9} = \sqrt{25} = 5 \text{ units}$$

To find the distance between points D and E, let $E(6, 5) = (x_1, y_1)$ and $D(2, 2) = (x_2, y_2)$.

$$DE = \sqrt{(6 - 2)^2 + (5 - 2)^2} = \sqrt{(4)^2 + (3)^2}$$
$$DE = \sqrt{16 + 9} = \sqrt{25} = 5 \text{ units}$$

Since $\triangle DEF$ and $\triangle HIG$ have the same shape and the same size, they are congruent.

Note: The Distance Formula is explained in more detail in Practice 24.

Similar Triangles

Two triangles are **similar** when they have the same shape (but not necessarily the same size). This means that when two triangles are similar, their vertices can be matched up so that corresponding angles (but not necessarily corresponding sides) are congruent. For example, $\triangle RST$ is similar to $\triangle HIJ$, denoted by $\triangle RST \sim \triangle HIJ$ (with corresponding vertices named in the same order).

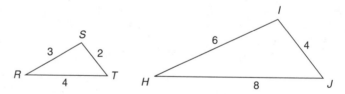

Corresponding angles are: $\angle R$ and $\angle H$; $\angle S$ and $\angle I$; $\angle T$ and $\angle J$.

Note: Congruent triangles are always similar. However, as the above example shows, similar triangles are not necessarily congruent.

Although the corresponding sides of similar triangles are not always congruent, the ratios of corresponding sides are equal. The ratio of two corresponding sides is called the **scale factor**. For example, in the diagram given above,

CORRESPONDING SIDES	SCALE FACTOR
$\overline{RS}$ and $\overline{HI}$	$\dfrac{RS}{HI} = \dfrac{3}{6} = \dfrac{1}{2}$
$\overline{ST}$ and $\overline{IJ}$	$\dfrac{ST}{IJ} = \dfrac{2}{4} = \dfrac{1}{2}$
$\overline{RT}$ and $\overline{HJ}$	$\dfrac{RT}{HJ} = \dfrac{4}{8} = \dfrac{1}{2}$

Model Problem 5   Are the triangles below similar?

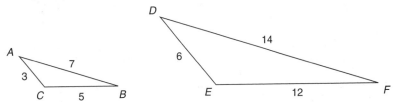

Solution   If △ACB ~ △DEF, corresponding sides must have equal ratios.

CORRESPONDING SIDES	SCALE FACTOR
$\overline{AC}$ and $\overline{DE}$	$\dfrac{AC}{DE} = \dfrac{3}{6} = \dfrac{1}{2}$
$\overline{AB}$ and $\overline{DF}$	$\dfrac{AB}{DF} = \dfrac{7}{14} = \dfrac{1}{2}$
$\overline{CB}$ and $\overline{EF}$	$\dfrac{CB}{EF} = \dfrac{5}{12}$

The corresponding sides do not have equal ratios; therefore, the triangles are not similar.

Model Problem 6   Refer to the diagram below, in which △ABC ~ △WYZ, and complete items **a** and **b**.

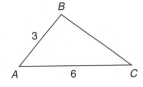 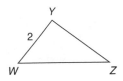

a If m∠W = 80°, then m∠A = _?_ .

b If AC = 6, then WZ = _?_ .

Solution   **a** m∠A = 80° because corresponding angles are congruent in similar triangles.

b These two triangles are similar, so the ratios of corresponding sides are equal; the scale factor is $\dfrac{3}{2}$. Thus,

$$\frac{AB}{WY} = \frac{AC}{WZ}$$

$$\frac{3}{2} = \frac{6}{WZ}$$

Solving for WZ, we get

$$3(WZ) = 6 \cdot 2$$

$$3(WZ) = 12$$

$$WZ = 4$$

Model Problem 7   Given: $\triangle ACD \sim \triangle ABE$.

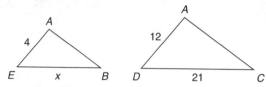

Find the value of x.

Solution   **Step 1.**   Separate the two triangles with their measures.

Step 2.   The scale factor of the smaller triangle to the larger triangle is $\frac{4}{12}$ or $\frac{1}{3}$ in reduced form.

Step 3.   Write a proportion showing the relationship between the scale factor, the missing side, and its corresponding side.

$$\frac{1}{3} = \frac{BE}{DC}$$
$$\frac{1}{3} = \frac{x}{21}$$
$$3x = 21$$
$$x = 7$$

Note: The ratio of the perimeters of two similar triangles is equal to the scale factor.

Model Problem 8   Given: $\triangle HIJ \sim \triangle PKQ$, the scale factor of the two triangles is $\frac{1}{3}$, and the perimeter of $\triangle HIJ$ is 12 centimeters.

Find the perimeter of $\triangle PKQ$, when

a $\triangle PKQ$ is the larger triangle.
b $\triangle PKQ$ is the smaller triangle.

Solution   **a** The scale factor: $\dfrac{\triangle HIJ}{\triangle PKQ} = \dfrac{1}{3}$.

$$\frac{\text{Perimeter of } \triangle HIJ}{\text{Perimeter of } \triangle PKQ} = \text{Scale factor}$$

$$\frac{12}{x} = \frac{1}{3}$$
$$x = 36$$

Therefore, the perimeter of $\triangle PKQ$ is 36 centimeters.

b The scale factor: $\dfrac{\triangle PKQ}{\triangle HIJ} = \dfrac{1}{3}$.

$$\frac{\text{Perimeter of } \triangle PKQ}{\text{Perimeter of } \triangle HIJ} = \text{Scale factor}$$

$$\frac{x}{12} = \frac{1}{3}$$
$$3x = 12$$
$$x = 4$$

Therefore, the perimeter of $\triangle PKQ$ is 4 centimeters.

1. Suppose that $\triangle ABC \cong \triangle DEF$ in the figure below.

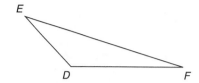

Complete the following.

a $\angle C \cong$?

b $\overline{AB} \cong$?

c $\overline{DF} \cong$?

d $\triangle CBA \cong$?

2. Determine if $\triangle KLM \cong \triangle PQR$.

$\triangle KLM$: $K(1, 3)$, $L(6, 6)$, and $M(4, 7)$.

$\triangle PQR$: $P(^-5, 1)$, $Q(^-10, 5)$, and $R(^-1, 1)$.

3. **Given:** $\triangle TOP \sim \triangle LMN$, m$\angle P = 90°$, and m$\angle O = 50°$.

Find m$\angle M$ and m$\angle L$.

4. Decide if $\triangle ABC$ and $\triangle FGH$ are similar.

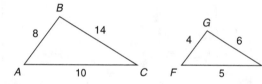

5. **Given:** $\triangle MOP \sim \triangle XYZ$.

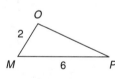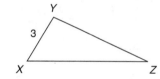

Find the length of $\overline{XZ}$.

6. **Given:** $\triangle ZPY \cong \triangle VPY$, $ZY = (2x + 5)$, and $VY = (3x - 7)$.

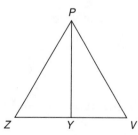

Find the length of $\overline{VY}$.

7. If $\triangle ABE \sim \triangle ACD$, find the value of x.

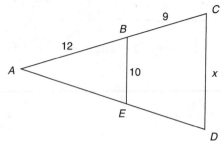

8. If $\triangle ACF \sim \triangle PQR$, $\triangle A = 60°$, and $\angle Q = 74°$, find $\angle R$.

ASSESSMENT

1. Given: $\triangle ABC \cong \triangle TOP$.

Which of the following correctly describes the relationship between the angles of $\triangle ABC$ and $\triangle TOP$?

A $\angle A \cong \angle O, \angle B \cong \angle T, \angle C \cong \angle P$

B $\angle A \cong \angle T, \angle B \cong \angle P, \angle C \cong \angle O$

C $\angle A \cong \angle P, \angle B \cong \angle O, \angle C \cong \angle T$

D $\angle A \cong \angle T, \angle B \cong \angle O, \angle C \cong \angle P$

2. Given: $\triangle BIG \sim \triangle CAT$.

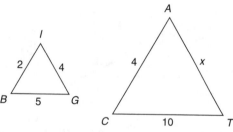

Find the value of x.

F 2

G 8

H 15

J 16

3. Given: $\triangle WXY \cong \triangle POQ$, $m\angle W = 70°$, and $m\angle Q = 50°$.

Find $m\angle X$.

A 70°

B 60°

C 50°

D 40°

4. Given: $\triangle ABP \sim \triangle DBC$.

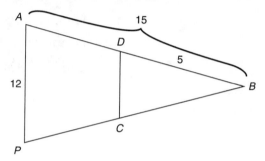

Find DC.

F 4

G 6

H 6.25

J 36

5.

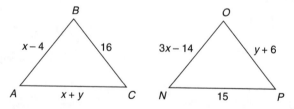

Find the value of x and y if $\triangle ABC \cong \triangle NOP$.

A $x = 12; y = 3$

B $x = 6; y = 9$

C $x = 5; y = 10$

D $x = 4; y = 11$

6. The scale factor of two similar triangles is $\frac{2}{3}$. If the larger triangle's perimeter is 66 centimeters, what is the perimeter of the smaller triangle?

   F 99

   G 88

   H 44

   J 10.8

For problems 7 and 8, use the diagram below where $\triangle RST \sim \triangle DEF$.

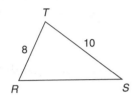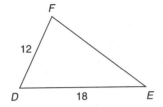

7. The scale factor is ? .

   F $\frac{4}{9}$

   G $\frac{2}{3}$

   H $\frac{4}{5}$

   J $\frac{5}{6}$

8. Find the length of $\overline{RS}$.

   A 27

   B 21.6

   C 18

   D 12

9. **Given:** $LK = 3$ cm, $NO = 15$ cm, $LM = 4$ cm, and $LN = 16$ cm.

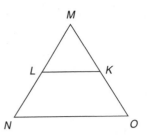

   If $\triangle MNO \sim \triangle MLK$, find the scale factor.

   F 1:5

   G 1:6

   H 3:4

   J 3:5

10. **Given:** $\triangle ABC \sim \triangle EDC$.

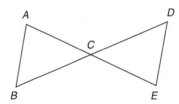

   Which of the following correctly describes the relationship between the sides of $\triangle ABC$ and $\triangle EDC$?

   A $\frac{AB}{BC} = \frac{AC}{ED} = \frac{BC}{EC}$

   B $\frac{AB}{ED} = \frac{BC}{DC} = \frac{AC}{EC}$

   C $\frac{AB}{EC} = \frac{BC}{ED} = \frac{AC}{DC}$

   D $\frac{AB}{BC} = \frac{AC}{ED} = \frac{BC}{DC}$

PRACTICE 10   Proving Triangles Congruent or Similar

Objective:	SOL G.5b

☐ The student will prove two triangles are congruent or similar, given information in the form of a figure or statement, using algebraic and coordinate as well as deductive proofs.

Proving Triangles Congruent   Practice 10 will discuss the five most common ways of proving (or showing) that two triangles are congruent. The table on the next page defines each method in detail.

METHOD	DESCRIPTION
Side-Side-Side (SSS) 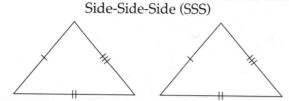	If three sides of one triangle are congruent to three sides of the other triangle, then the triangles are congruent.
Side-Angle-Side (SAS) 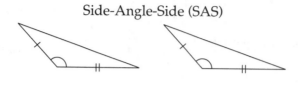	If two sides and the included angle of one triangle are congruent to two sides and the included angle of the other triangle, then the triangles are congruent.
Angle-Side-Angle (ASA) 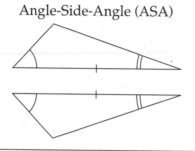	If two angles and the included side of one triangle are congruent to two angles and the included side of the other triangle, then the triangles are congruent.
Angle-Angle-Side (AAS) 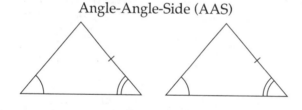	If two angles and a non-included side of one triangle are congruent to two angles and a non-included side of the other triangle, then the triangles are congruent.
Hypotenuse-Leg (HL) 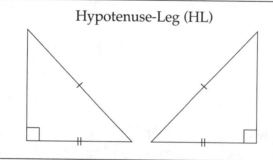	If the hypotenuse and a leg of one *right* triangle are congruent to the hypotenuse and a leg of the other *right* triangle, then the triangles are congruent.

The following table summarizes these methods:

TWO TRIANGLES ARE CONGRUENT WHEN THESE CORRESPONDING PARTS ARE CONGRUENT:

SSS	3 sides
SAS	2 sides and the included angle
ASA	2 angles and the included side
AAS	2 angles and a non-included side
HL	hypotenuse and leg (right triangles only)

Model Problem 1   Use the markings on the two triangles to determine if the triangles are congruent.

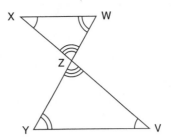

Solution   **Method 1 (if *not* drawn to scale)**
All you know about the two triangles is that corresponding angles are congruent (Angle-Angle-Angle or AAA). Unfortunately, AAA does not prove that two triangles are congruent. Therefore, we do not have enough information to conclude that the triangles are congruent.

Method 2 (if drawn to scale)
Step 1.   Draw $\triangle VYZ$ on a sheet of patty paper including all of its markings.
Step 2.   Match the markings of $\triangle VYZ$ with the markings of $\triangle XWZ$.
Step 3.   These triangles are not the same size. Therefore, $\triangle VYZ$ is not congruent to $\triangle XWZ$.

**TWO TRIANGLES ARE *NOT* (NECESSARILY) CONGRUENT
WHEN THESE CORRESPONDING PARTS ARE CONGRUENT:**

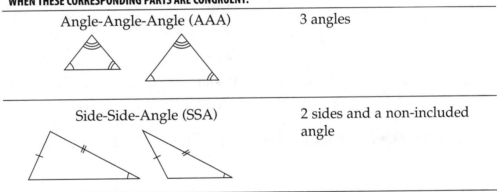

| Angle-Angle-Angle (AAA) | 3 angles |
| Side-Side-Angle (SSA) | 2 sides and a non-included angle |

Thus, when you are *only* given AAA or SSA on a diagram, do *not* conclude that the triangles are congruent.

Model Problem 2   Explain why these two triangles are congruent.

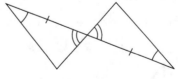

Solution   The tick marks indicate that two angles and the included side of one triangle are congruent to two angles and the included side of the other triangle (ASA). Therefore, the triangles are congruent by ASA.

Model Problem 3

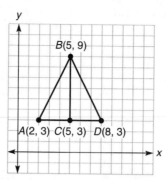

Use algebraic and coordinate methods to show $\triangle ABC \cong \triangle DBC$.

Solution $\overline{BC}$ and $\overline{AD}$ are perpendicular because they are gridlines. Hence, $\triangle ABC$ and $\triangle DBC$ are right triangles. Therefore, we need to show that the hypotenuse and a leg of one triangle are congruent to the hypotenuse and a leg of the other triangle (HL).

Step 1. $\overline{BC} \cong \overline{BC}$ by the reflexive property of congruency.

Step 2.   Use the distance formula, $d = \sqrt{(x_2 - x_1)^2 + (y_2 - y_1)^2}$, to show that the hypotenuses are congruent.

Let $A(2, 3) = (x_1, y_1)$ and $B(5, 9) = (x_2, y_2)$.	Let $B(5, 9) = (x_1, y_1)$ and $D(8, 3) = (x_2, y_2)$.
$AB = \sqrt{(5 - 2)^2 + (9 - 3)^2}$	$BD = \sqrt{(8 - 5)^2 + (3 - 9)^2}$
$AB = \sqrt{(3)^2 + (6)^2}$	$BD = \sqrt{(3)^2 + (^-6)^2}$
$AB = \sqrt{9 + 36}$	$BD = \sqrt{9 + 36}$
$AB = \sqrt{45}$	$BD = \sqrt{45}$

Thus, $\overline{AB} \cong \overline{BD}$.

Step 3.   Therefore, by HL, $\triangle ABC \cong \triangle DBC$.

Model Problem 4   Given: $\overline{AB} \cong \overline{AC}$, and $\overline{AM}$ bisects $\angle BAC$.

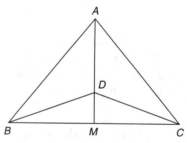

Prove $\triangle BAD \cong \triangle CAD$.

Solution   Step 1.   Use the given statements and the diagram to find congruent corresponding parts.

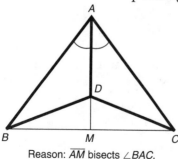

Reason: $\overline{AM}$ bisects $\angle BAC$, so $\angle BAD \cong \angle CAD$

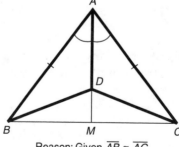

Reason: Given $\overline{AB} \cong \overline{AC}$, so $\overline{AB} \cong \overline{AC}$

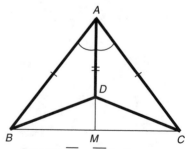

Reason: $\overline{AD} \cong \overline{AD}$ by the reflexive property of congruency

Step 2.   Therefore, by Side-Angle-Side (SAS), $\triangle BAD \cong \triangle CAD$.

Proving Triangles Similar   Two triangles can be proven similar by using one of the following methods, Angle-Angle, Side-Angle-Side, or Side-Side-Side. The table below explains each of these methods.

REMEMBER

Congruent triangles are always similar, but the opposite is not necessarily true, that is, similar triangles are not always congruent.

METHOD	SYMBOL	DESCRIPTION
Angle-Angle	AA~	If two angles of one triangle are congruent to two angles of the other triangle, then the triangles are similar. Also known as AAA~.
Side-Angle-Side	SAS~	If an angle of one triangle is congruent to an angle of the other, and the sides including these angles have the same ratio, then the triangles are similar.
Side-Side-Side	SSS~	If corresponding sides have the same ratio, then the two triangles are similar.

Model Problem 5   Show that Triangle I is similar to Triangle II.

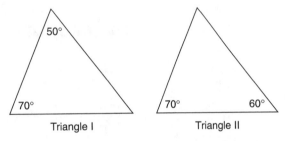

Solution   Step 1.   The missing angle in Triangle I is 60° since the sum of the angles in a triangle is 180°.

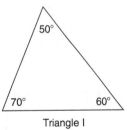

Step 2.   Compare the angles in Triangle I to the angles in Triangle II. Two angles in Triangle I are congruent to two angles in Triangle II.

Step 3.   Therefore, by AA~, Triangle I is similar to Triangle II.

Model Problem 6   Determine if $\triangle EDF \sim \triangle IHJ$. If so, state why.

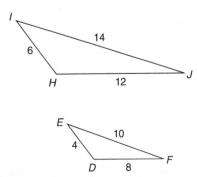

Solution   Step 1.   If these triangles are similar, then their corresponding sides must have the same ratio, that is, $\frac{ED}{IH} = \frac{DF}{HJ} = \frac{FE}{JI}$.

Step 2.   Find the ratios.

$$\frac{ED}{IH} = \frac{4}{6} = \frac{2}{3} \qquad \frac{DF}{HJ} = \frac{8}{12} = \frac{2}{3} \qquad \frac{FE}{JI} = \frac{10}{14} = \frac{5}{7}$$

Step 3.   The ratios are not all the same. Therefore, $\triangle EDF$ is not similar to $\triangle IHJ$.

The concept of similar triangles can be used to solve many problems in the real world such as shadow and projection problems.

Example

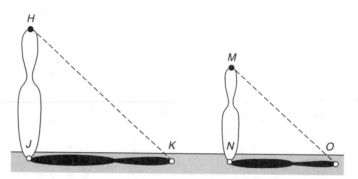

Show that the triangles formed by the two nearby objects, the ground, and the light rays ($\triangle HJK$ and $\triangle MNO$) are similar.

Note: In shadow and projection problems, assume that the ground is level and that objects are vertical to the ground. Also, assume that light rays hitting nearby objects are parallel to each other.

Solution

Step 1.   Since the objects are vertical to the ground, they form 90° angles with the ground.

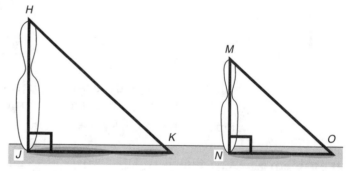

Step 2.   Since the light rays are parallel, they cut the objects at congruent angles.

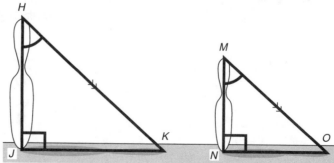

Step 3.   Therefore, the two triangles are similar by AA~.

   This relationship is true for any pair of nearby objects, and we record this as a rule.

> **RULE:** In shadow problems, triangles formed by nearby objects, the ground, and light rays are similar.

Model Problem 7   Brian notices that a 25-meter flagpole casts a 30-meter shadow. If a nearby telephone pole casts a 40-meter shadow, how tall is the telephone pole?

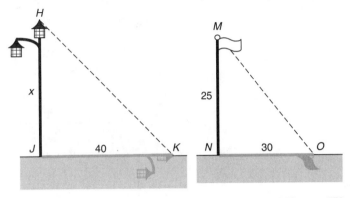

Solution $\triangle HJK \sim \triangle MNO$ by the "shadow problem" rule. Thus, $\dfrac{HJ}{MN} = \dfrac{JK}{NO}$.

$$\frac{x}{25} = \frac{40}{30}$$

$$x = 33\frac{1}{3}$$

Therefore, the telephone pole is $33\frac{1}{3}$ meters tall.

TRY THESE

1.

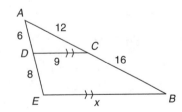

Find the value of x.

2.

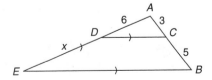

What is the value of x?

3. **Given:** $\overline{FH}$ bisects $\angle GFJ$ and $\angle GHJ$.

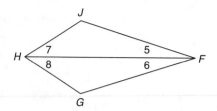

   Why is $\triangle GFH$ congruent to $\triangle JFH$?

4. Which pair of triangles must be similar?

   A

   B

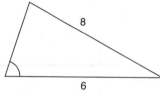

   C

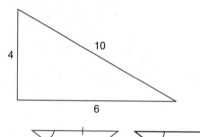

   D

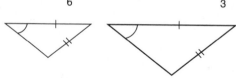

5. **Given:** $BI = 12$ inches, $ID = 5$ inches, $IC = 7$ inches.

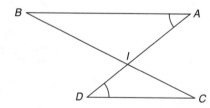

   Find AI.

6. **Given:** $\overline{EH} \cong \overline{EG}$, and $\overline{EF} \cong \overline{EI}$.

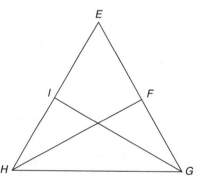

   Why is $\triangle EIG \cong \triangle EFH$?

7.

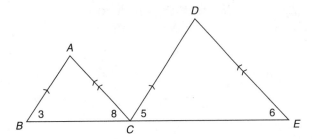

Prove $\triangle ABC \sim \triangle DCE$.

ASSESSMENT

1. If $\angle W \cong \angle Y$ and $\frac{XW}{TY} = \frac{WZ}{YU}$, state the reason $\triangle XWZ \sim \triangle TYU$.

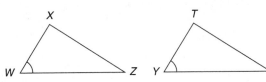

A ASA

B SSS

C AA

D SAS

2. Why is $\triangle QKI$ congruent to $\triangle PNM$?

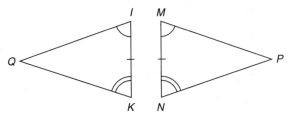

F Side-Angle-Side (SAS)

G Side-Side-Angle (SSA)

H Angle-Angle-Angle (AAA)

J Angle-Side-Angle (ASA)

3. Why are these two triangles similar?

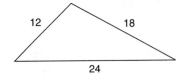

A SAS

B SSA

C SSS

D ASA

4. To prove $\triangle XYZ \cong \triangle UWV$ by HL, which additional pair of parts must be congruent?

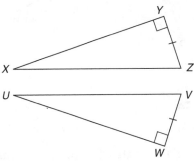

F $\overline{XY}$ and $\overline{UW}$

G $\overline{XZ}$ and $\overline{UV}$

H $\angle YXZ$ and $\angle WUV$

J $\angle YXZ$ and $\angle WVU$

5. Which could be used to prove $\triangle BAC \sim \triangle DEC$?

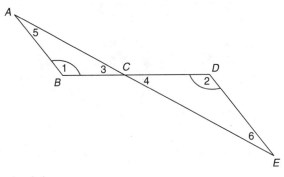

A AA~

B ASA~

C AAS~

D SAS~

6. To prove $\triangle GIH \sim \triangle JKP$ by SAS, which additional pair of parts must be congruent?

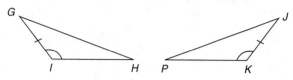

F $\overline{GH}$ and $\overline{JP}$

G $\angle H$ and $\angle P$

H $\overline{GH}$ and $\overline{PK}$

J $\overline{HI}$ and $\overline{PK}$

7. Which could be used to prove $\triangle ABC \sim \triangle EBF$?

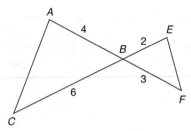

A SSS~

B SAS~

C SSA~

D AA~

8. What coordinates for point T would make $\triangle FGH$ congruent to $\triangle RAT$?

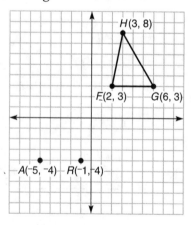

F (⁻4, 0)

G (⁻2, 1)

H (⁻3, 1)

J (⁻2, ⁻7)

9. What is the length of $\overline{MN}$ that makes $\triangle KMN$ similar to $\triangle QPN$?

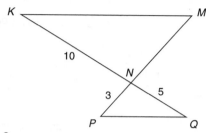

A $\frac{3}{2}$

B 3

C 6

D $16\frac{2}{3}$

10.

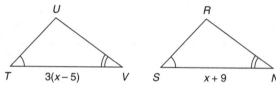

The two triangles are congruent when the value of x is —

F 12

G 7

H 6

J 3

PRACTICE 11 Triangle Inequality (Lengths of Sides and the Measures of Angles)

Objective:	SOL G.6

❑ The student, given information concerning the lengths of sides and/or measures of angles, will apply the triangle inequality properties to determine whether a triangle exists and to order sides and angles. These concepts will be considered in the context of practical situations.

There are many combinations of lengths that can be used to form a triangle. A triangle can be formed from three segments if the sum of the lengths of *any* two segments is greater than the length of the third segment.

Test Tip

To determine if a triangle can be formed from three segments, you need *only* add the lengths of the two smaller segments first, and compare the sum to the length of the remaining segment. If the sum is greater, then you can form a triangle; otherwise, a triangle cannot be formed.

Model Problem 1   Does a triangle with sides of length 3, 8, and 12 exist?

Solution   The sum of the two shortest sides must be greater than the longest side.

Is $\underbrace{3 + 8}_{\substack{\text{sum of the} \\ \text{smaller lengths}}}$ = 11 > $\underbrace{12}_{\substack{\text{largest} \\ \text{length}}}$?   No.

Therefore, such a triangle does not exist.

The Relationship Between the Sides and the Angles of a Triangle

- The shortest side of a triangle is opposite the smallest angle of the triangle, and the longest side is opposite the largest angle.
- The smallest angle of a triangle is opposite the shortest side of the triangle, and the largest angle is opposite the longest side.
- Given any two sides of a triangle, the length of the third side is greater than the difference and less than the sum of the lengths of the two given sides.

Model Problem 2   Arrange the angles of $\triangle JIG$ in order from smallest to largest.

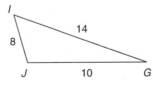

Solution   Step 1.   The smallest angle is opposite the shortest side. $\overline{JI}$ is the shortest side, so $\angle G$ is the smallest angle.

Step 2.   The largest angle is opposite the longest side. $\overline{IG}$ is the longest side, so $\angle J$ is the largest angle.

Step 3.   Therefore, $\angle G$, $\angle I$, $\angle J$ is the correct order from smallest to largest.

Model Problem 3

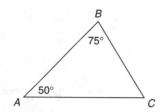

List the sides of △ABC in order from shortest to longest.

Solution Step 1. The missing angle in the triangle is 55°, because the sum of the angles in a triangle is 180°.

Step 2. The shortest side is opposite the smallest angle. ∠A is the smallest angle, so $\overline{BC}$ is the shortest side.

Step 3. The longest side is opposite the largest angle. ∠B is the largest angle, so $\overline{AC}$ is the longest side.

Step 4. Therefore, $\overline{BC}$, $\overline{AB}$, $\overline{AC}$ is the correct order from shortest to longest.

Model Problem 4 Two sides of a triangle have lengths 9 and 16. The length of the third side must be greater than ? and less than ? .

Solution The length of the missing side is greater than the difference (16 − 9 = 7) and less than the sum (16 + 9 = 25) of the lengths of the two given sides, or

$$\underbrace{16 - 9 = 7}_{\text{difference}} < \text{length of the third side} < \underbrace{16 + 9 = 25}_{\text{sum}}$$

Therefore, the length of the third side must be greater than 7 and less than 25.

TRY THESE

1. List the angles of △ABC from smallest to largest.

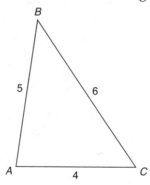

2. Is it possible for a triangle to have sides with lengths 10, 9, and 8?

3. Arrange the sides of △RST in order from shortest to longest.

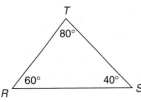

4. Two sides of a triangle have lengths 10 and 4. The length of the third side must be greater than ? and less than ? .

5. Is it possible for a triangle to have sides with lengths 7, 7, and 14?

6.

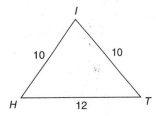

Name the largest angle.

ASSESSMENT

1. Which of the following can be the lengths of the sides of a triangle?

   A 1, 2, 4

   B 1, 6, 7

   C 4, 5, 11

   D 8, 9, 13

2.

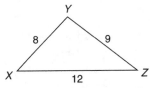

From smallest to largest, the angles of △XYZ are —

F ∠X, ∠Y, ∠Z

G ∠Y, ∠Z, ∠X

H ∠Z, ∠X, ∠Y

J ∠Z, ∠Y, ∠X

3. From home, Brett walked northeast 5 miles to an old tree stump. He walked southeast an additional 2 miles to the lake. Which is a possible distance between Brett's house and the lake?

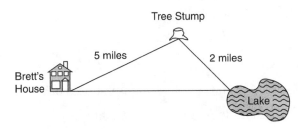

A 10 miles

B 7 miles

C 5 miles

D 3 miles

4.

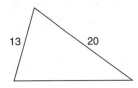

Which of the following is a possible length for the third side of the triangle?

F 7

G 19

H 33

J 35

5.

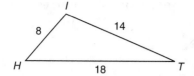

Which lists the angles in order from largest to smallest?

A ∠I, ∠H, and ∠T

B ∠I, ∠T, and ∠H

C ∠H, ∠I, and ∠T

D ∠H, ∠T, and ∠I

6. Given: △XYZ.

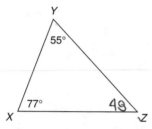

Which of the following is true?

F $\overline{XY} < \overline{XZ} < \overline{YZ}$

G $\overline{XY} < \overline{YZ} < \overline{XZ}$

H $\overline{XZ} < \overline{YZ} < \overline{XY}$

J $\overline{YZ} < \overline{XZ} < \overline{XY}$

7. Given: △XYZ, and XZ < YZ.

Which of the following must be true?

A Angle X is smaller than angle Y.

B Angle X is smaller than angle Z.

C Angle Y is smaller than angle X.

D Angle Y is smaller than angle Z.

8. A flower bed in the City Park is designed to be in the shape of a triangle. An evergreen tree will be planted in the largest corner.

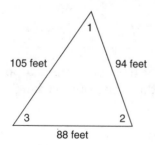

In which corner will the evergreen tree be planted?

F ∠1

G ∠2

H ∠3

J ∠4

9. A crane at a construction site has a boom that is 350 feet and a mast of 120 feet.

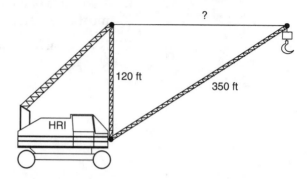

What is the maximum length of the cable wire to the nearest foot?

A 228 ft.

B 230 ft.

C 469 ft.

D 470 ft.

10. Three trees mark the perimeter of a lot.

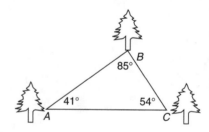

Which lists the distances between the trees in order from least to greatest?

F AB, BC, and AC

G AC, AB, and BC

H AC, BC, and AB

J BC, AB, and AC

PRACTICE 12   Right Triangles

Objective:	SOL G.7

☐ The student will solve practical problems involving right triangles by using the Pythagorean Theorem, properties of special right triangles, and right triangle trigonometry. Solutions will be expressed in radical form or as decimal approximations.

The study of right triangles will begin by identifying the parts of a right triangle. In a right triangle, the side opposite the right angle is called the **hypotenuse** and the other two sides are called the **legs**.

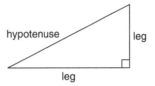

Pythagorean Theorem A Greek mathematician, Pythagoras, developed one of the best-known and most useful theorems concerning the relationship between the hypotenuse and the two legs of a right triangle; this theorem is known as the **Pythagorean Theorem**.

Pythagorean Theorem

In a right triangle, the sum of the squares of the legs is equal to the square of the hypotenuse. In symbols, if a and b are the lengths of the two legs, and c is the length of the hypotenuse, then $a^2 + b^2 = c^2$

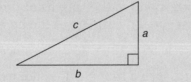

$$a^2 + b^2 = c^2$$

Model Problem 1 A 25-foot ladder leans against a house. How far is the top of the ladder from the ground if the foot of the ladder is 15 feet from the base of the building?

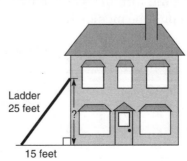

Ladder
25 feet

15 feet

Solution Step 1. Draw and label the triangle with x representing the distance from the top of the ladder to the ground.

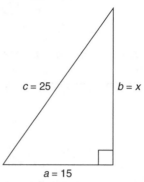

Step 2. Use the Pythagorean Theorem, $a^2 + b^2 = c^2$, with $a = 15$, $b = x$, and $c = 25$, and solve for x.

$$15^2 + x^2 = 25^2$$
$$225 + x^2 = 625$$
$$x^2 = 625 - 225 = 400$$
$$x = \sqrt{400} = 20$$

TI KEYSTROKES

ON CLEAR 25 x^2 − 15 x^2 ENTER 2nd x^2 400 ENTER

CASIO KEYSTROKES

AC/ON 25 x^2 − 15 x^2 EXE SHIFT x^2 400 EXE

Therefore, the top of the ladder is 20 feet above the ground.

Model Problem 2 Does a right triangle with sides of lengths 5, 12, and 14 exist?

Solution Since the hypotenuse is the longest side of a right triangle, the largest number must correspond to the length of the hypotenuse (and the other two numbers must correspond to the lengths of the two legs.) The sum of the squares of the legs must equal the square of the hypotenuse.

Is $5^2 + 12^2 = 14^2$? No, since $5^2 + 12^2 = 169$ and $14^2 = 196$.

Therefore, such a triangle does not exist.

Properties of Special Right Triangles The special geometric properties of 30°-60°-90° right triangles and 45°-45°-90° right triangles are summarized in the table below. These relationships are not on the formula sheet; however, they may appear on the test. Therefore, they should be memorized before taking the SOL test.

TYPE OF TRIANGLE	SHAPE OF TRIANGLE	PROPERTIES
30°-60°-90° (short leg is opposite the 30°angle) (long leg is opposite the 60°angle)	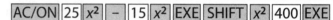	hypotenuse = short leg · 2 long leg = short leg · $\sqrt{3}$

TYPE OF TRIANGLE	SHAPE OF TRIANGLE	PROPERTIES
45°-45°-90° (each leg has the same length)	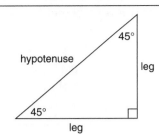	$\text{hypotenuse} = \text{leg} \cdot \sqrt{2}$ $\text{leg} = \dfrac{\text{hypotenuse}}{2} \cdot \sqrt{2}$

Model Problem 3   A 34-foot ladder leaning against a wall makes an angle of 60° with the ground. How high up the wall does the ladder reach?

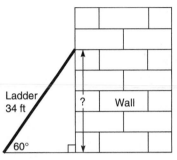

Solution   Step 1.   Draw and label the triangle.

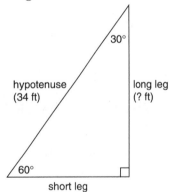

Step 2.   Use the formula for 30°-60°-90° triangles involving the long leg.

$$\text{long leg} = \text{short leg} \cdot \sqrt{3}$$

Step 3.   Since we are not given the length of the short leg, we will need to use the other formula for 30°-60°-90° triangles to determine this length.

$$\text{hypotenuse} = \text{short leg} \cdot 2$$
$$34 = \text{short leg} \cdot 2$$
$$17 = \text{short leg}$$

Step 4.   Use this value to find the length of the long leg.

$$\text{long leg} = \text{short leg} \cdot \sqrt{3}$$
$$x = 17\sqrt{3}$$

Therefore, the ladder reaches $17\sqrt{3}$ feet or approximately 29.4 feet up the side of the wall.

Model Problem 4 The brace used to support a mailbox has broken off and needs to be replaced. Find the length of the replacement brace.

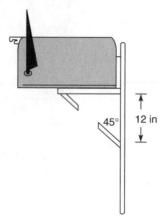

Solution Step 1. Draw and label the triangle.

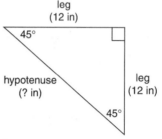

Step 2. In a 45°-45°-90° triangle,

$$\text{hypotenuse} = \text{short leg} \cdot \sqrt{2}$$
$$x = 12$$
$$x \approx 16.97$$

Therefore, the brace is $12\sqrt{2}$ inches or approximately 16.97 inches long.

Right Triangle Trigonometry Trigonometric ratios to remember:

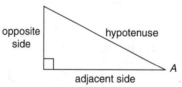

$$\sin \angle A = \frac{\text{opposite side}}{\text{hypotenuse}}$$

$$\cos \angle A = \frac{\text{adjacent side}}{\text{hypotenuse}}$$

$$\tan \angle A = \frac{\text{opposite side}}{\text{adjacent side}}$$

Test Tip

Memorizing the short phrase **SOH-CAH-TOA** will help you remember the trigonometric ratios.

Sin = **O**pposite over **H**ypotenuse	(SOH)
Cos = **A**djacent over **H**ypotenuse	(CAH)
Tan = **O**pposite over **A**djacent	(TOA)

Model Problem 5   A lighthouse casts a 30-meter shadow when the angle of elevation of the sun is 38°.

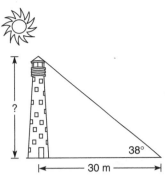

How tall is the lighthouse?

Solution   Identify the trigonometric ratio represented in this problem. Use the ratio involving the tan function since we are given the lengths of one of the legs and the measure of an acute angle.

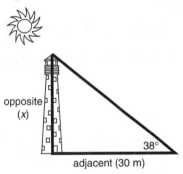

$$\tan \angle A = \frac{\text{opposite side}}{\text{adjacent side}}$$

$$\tan 38° = \frac{x}{30}$$

$$30 \cdot \tan 38° = x$$

TI KEYSTROKES

ON | MODE | ▼ | ▼ | ▶ | ENTER | CLEAR | 30 | × | TAN | 38 | ENTER

CASIO KEYSTROKES

1 | SHIFT | MENU | ▼ | ▼ | F1 | QUIT | TAN | 38 | × | 30 | EXE

Therefore, the lighthouse is approximately 23.4 meters tall.

Note: If the question has the angle measurement in degrees, make sure the calculator is in degree mode. If the question has the angle measurement in radians, make sure the calculator is in radian mode.

Model Problem 6   Find the measure of x to the nearest degree.

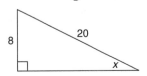

Solution   Identify the trigonometric ratio represented in the problem.

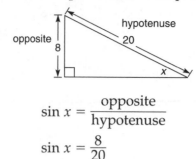

$$\sin x = \frac{\text{opposite}}{\text{hypotenuse}}$$

$$\sin x = \frac{8}{20}$$

TI KEYSTROKES

CASIO KEYSTROKES

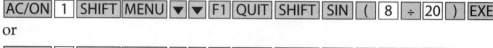

or

| AC/ON | 1 | SHIFT | MENU | ▼ | ▼ | F1 | QUIT | SHIFT | SIN | 8 | / | 20 | EXE |

Therefore, the measure of x to the nearest degree is 24°.

 T R Y   T H E S E

1. An equilateral triangle has sides of length 18. Find the length of one altitude to the nearest tenth.

Note: An **altitude** of a triangle is the line segment from a vertex, perpendicular to the opposite side. In equilateral triangles, the altitudes are all congruent.

2. Baseball diamonds are square-shaped. Find the distance between first base and third base to the nearest hundredth of a foot if each side of the baseball diamond is 90 feet.

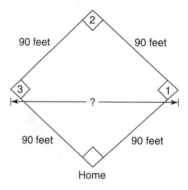

3. The perimeter of a square is 48 centimeters. Find the length of each diagonal.

   Hint: The perimeter of a square = 4 · side.

4. Find the value of x in the triangle below.

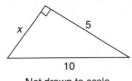

Not drawn to scale.

5. Find the height of the tree to the nearest foot.

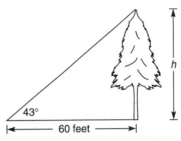

6.

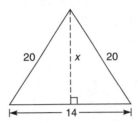

Find the length of the altitude, x, to the nearest hundredth of a meter.
Hint: The given altitude bisects the base.

7. Find the value of x to the nearest degree.

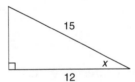

  ASSESSMENT

1. What is the length of a diagonal of a square with a perimeter of 28 centimeters?

   A 7
   B $7\sqrt{2}$
   C $7\sqrt{3}$
   D 49

2.

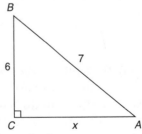

The value of x is —

   F $\sqrt{13}$
   G $\sqrt{85}$
   H 13
   J 85

3. The angle of elevation of the top of the flag-pole is 39°. How high is the flagpole if $WQ = $ 70 feet?

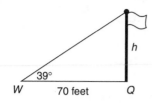

A 44.1 feet

B 54.4 feet

C 56.7 feet

D 86.4 feet

4. The measure of the angle of elevation of the sun is 32° when a building casts a shadow 250 feet long. How tall is the building to the nearest tenth of a foot?

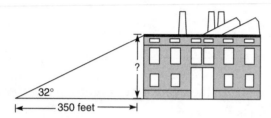

F 185.5 ft

G 218.7 ft

H 296.8 ft

J 560.1 ft

5. Find the value of x to the nearest degree.

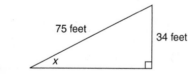

A 63°

B 27°

C 24°

D 21°

6. The captain of a small boat spots a light-house at an angle of elevation of 5°. If the lighthouse is 250 feet high, what is the distance between the boat and the lighthouse to the nearest tenth of a foot?

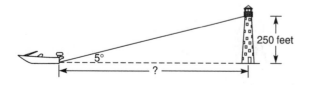

F 251.0 feet

G 298.0 feet

H 2,857.0 feet

J 2,857.5 feet

7. Edward would like to construct a right tri-angle out of drinking straws. The lengths of the hypotenuse and one of the legs are 17 and 8 centimeters, respectively. What must be the length of the other leg?

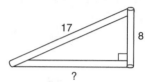

A 3 cm

B 9 cm

C 15 cm

D 25 cm

8. A piece of glass in a shape of a triangle is shown in the figure below.

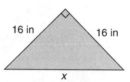

How long is the missing side?

F $4\sqrt{2}$ in

G 16 in

H $16\sqrt{2}$ in

J $16\sqrt{3}$ in

9. Find the value of x in the diagram below.

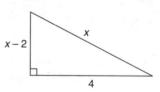

A 5

B 3

C ⁻3

D ⁻5

10. A ladder is leaning against a tree. If the foot of the ladder is 9 feet from the base of the tree and makes a 60° angle with the ground, what is the length of the ladder?

F $9\sqrt{2}$ ft
G $9\sqrt{3}$ ft
H 18 ft
J $18\sqrt{3}$ ft

11. Which list of numbers can be the lengths of the sides of a right triangle?

A 10, 12, 12
B 8, 15, 16
C $7, 7, 7\sqrt{2}$
D $7, 7, 7\sqrt{3}$

PRACTICE 13 Cumulative Practice on SOLs G.1a-d, 5a-b, 6, and 7

1. Which is the converse of the statement, "If you are at least 18 years old, then you need to register with selective service"?

   A If you are at least 18 years old, then you do not need to register with selective service.

   B If you do not need to register with selective service, then you are not at least 18 years old.

   C If you need to register with selective service, then you are at least 18 years old.

   D If you need to register with selective service, then you are not at least 18 years old.

2. Which of the following can be the lengths of the sides of a triangle?

   F 1, 4, 6
   G 1, 7, 9
   H 2, 2, 4
   J 15, 20, 25

3. What is the contrapositive of the statement, "If $x = 3$, then $3x + 10 = 19$"?

   A If $x = 3$, then $3x + 10 = 19$.
   B If $x \neq 3$, then $3x + 10 \neq 19$.
   C If $3x + 10 = 19$, then $x \neq 3$.
   D If $3x + 10 \neq 19$, then $x \neq 3$.

4. Which is the inverse of the statement, "If two angles are vertical angles, then they do not form a linear pair"?

   F If two angles form a linear pair, then they are not vertical angles.

   G If two angles are not vertical angles, then they form a linear pair.

   H If two angles do not form a linear pair, then they are vertical angles.

   J If two angles are vertical angles, then they form a linear pair.

5. Given: $\triangle ABC \cong \triangle TOP$.
   Which of the following is true?

   A $\overline{BC} \cong \overline{PO}; \overline{AC} \cong \overline{PT}; \overline{AB} \cong \overline{OT}$
   B $\overline{AC} \cong \overline{TP}; \overline{AB} \cong \overline{TO}; \overline{BC} \cong \overline{OP}$
   C $\overline{AC} \cong \overline{TO}; \overline{AB} \cong \overline{PO}; \overline{BC} \cong \overline{TP}$
   D $\overline{AB} \cong \overline{OP}; \overline{AC} \cong \overline{TP}; \overline{BC} \cong \overline{OT}$

6. Let p represent "$2x + 2 = 12$."
   Let q represent "$x = 5$."
   The symbolic form of the statement, "If $2x + 2 = 12$, then $x = 5$," is

   F $\sim p \rightarrow \sim q$
   G $p \rightarrow q$
   H $p \wedge q$
   J $p \vee q$

7. Let p represent "Linda can go."
    Let q represent "Scott can not go."
    The symbolic form of the statement, "If Scott can go, then Linda cannot go," is

    A $\sim q \rightarrow \sim p$

    B $\sim p \rightarrow \sim q$

    C $p \rightarrow q$

    D $q \rightarrow p$

8. The scale factor of two similar triangles is $\frac{2}{5}$.
    If the perimeter of the smaller triangle is 80 cm, what is the perimeter of the larger triangle?

    F 200 cm

    G 112 cm

    H 57 cm

    J 32 cm

9. Let d represent "A number is divisible by 2."
    Let n represent "It is divisible by 6."
    Which is the inverse of the statement, "If a number is divisible by 2, then it is divisible by 6," in symbolic form?

    A $\sim n \rightarrow \sim d$

    B $\sim d \rightarrow \sim n$

    C $d \rightarrow n$

    D $n \rightarrow d$

10. **Given:** $\triangle MNO \sim \triangle MLK$ with $LK = 3$ cm, $NO = 12$ cm, $LM = 6$ cm, and $LN = 18$ cm.

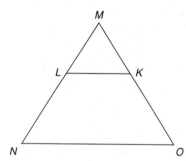

    Find the scale factor of the two triangles.

    F 4 to 1

    G 3 to 5

    H 3 to 4

    J 1 to 5

11. Which conclusion logically follows the true statements?
    "If x is negative, then $x < 0$."
    "If $x < 0$, then x^3 is negative."

    A If x is negative, then x^3 is negative.

    B If x is not negative, then $x < 0$.

    C x is negative.

    D x^3 is negative.

12. Which diagram represents the statement, "All Lincolns are made by Ford"?

    F
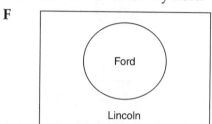

    G
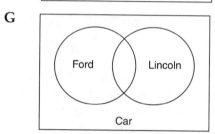

    H
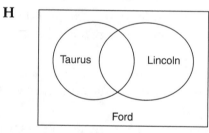

    J
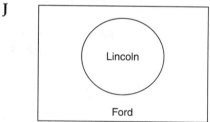

13. Which conclusion logically follows the true statements?
    "If you live in Richmond, then you live in Virginia."
    "You live in Richmond."

    A You do not live in Richmond.

    B You do not live in Virginia.

    C You live in Virginia.

    D If you live in Virginia, then you live in Richmond.

14. Given: △BIG ~ △CAT.

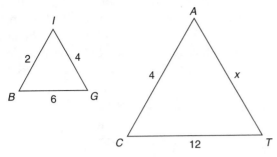

Find the value of *x*.

F 2

G 8

H 15

J 16

15. Given: △ABP ~ △DBC with AB = 15, DB = 5, and DC = 3.

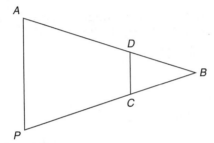

Find *AP*.

A 4

B 9

C 12

D 36

16. Let *r* represent "Today is Tuesday."
Let *s* represent "Tomorrow is Friday."
The symbolic form of the statement, "Today is Tuesday and tomorrow is not Friday," is

F $r \wedge s$

G $r \wedge \sim s$

H $\sim r \wedge s$

J $\sim r \wedge \sim s$

17. Given: △RST ~ △DEF.

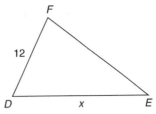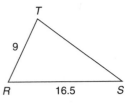

Find the length of $\overline{DE}$.

A 91.5

B 22

C 18

D 12.38

18. Let *p* represent "You start school at 7:30 AM."
Let *q* represent "You start school at 8:00 AM."
Which is the symbolic form of the statement, "You start school at 7:30 AM or you start school at 8:00 AM"?

F $p \wedge q$

G $\sim p \vee \sim q$

H $p \vee q$

J $\sim p \vee \sim q$

19. Which could be used to prove △QKI ≅ △PNM?

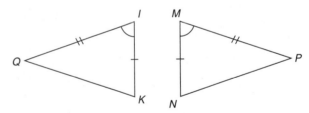

A Side-Angle-Side (SAS)

B Angle-Angle-Side (AAS)

C Angle-Angle-Angle (AAA)

D Side-Side-Angle (SSA)

20. Why are the two triangles similar in the diagram below?

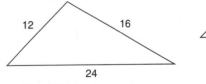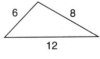

F ASA~

G SAS~

H SSA~

J SSS~

21. To prove △GIH ≅ △JKP by ASA, which additional pair of parts must be congruent?

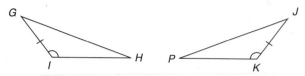

  A $\overline{GH}$ and $\overline{JP}$
  B ∠H and ∠P
  C ∠G and ∠J
  D $\overline{HI}$ and $\overline{PK}$

22. What is the converse of the statement, "If you pay for the pizza, then I'll pay for the buffalo wings"?

  F If I pay for the buffalo wings, then you pay for the pizza.
  G If I don't pay for the buffalo wings, then you don't pay for the pizza.
  H If you don't pay for the pizza, then I won't pay for the buffalo wings.
  J If you pay for the pizza, then I won't pay for the buffalo wings.

23. Which lists the angles in order from smallest to largest?

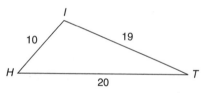

  A ∠I, ∠T, and ∠H
  B ∠H, ∠T, and ∠I
  C ∠H, ∠I, and ∠T
  D ∠T, ∠H, and ∠I

24. A model rocket is launched and hits a tree at a height of 25 meters above the ground before dropping straight down to the ground. If the rocket lands 15 meters from the launch site, what is the total distance traveled by the model rocket before it hits the tree?

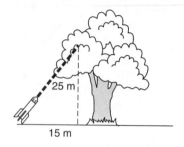

  F 40 meters
  G 20 meters
  H $5\sqrt{35}$ meters
  J $5\sqrt{34}$ meters

25. The measure of the angle of elevation of the sun is 60° when a building casts a shadow 400 feet long.

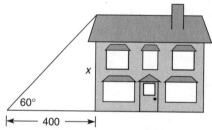

How tall is the building?

  A 400 feet
  B $400\sqrt{2}$ feet
  C $400\sqrt{3}$ feet
  D 800 feet

UNIT 3
Polygons and Circles

PRACTICE 14   Identifying Properties of Quadrilaterals

Objective:	SOL G.8a

☐ The student will investigate and identify properties of quadrilaterals involving opposite sides and angles, consecutive sides and angles, and diagonals.

A **quadrilateral** is a four-sided polygon. The following table gives the definitions of each type of quadrilateral and shows examples of each.

NAME	EXAMPLE	DEFINITION
Parallelogram		A quadrilateral with opposite sides congruent and parallel.
Rectangle		A parallelogram with four right angles.
Rhombus		A parallelogram with four congruent sides.

(continued)

NAME	EXAMPLE	DEFINITION
Square		A parallelogram with four right angles and four congruent sides.
Kite		A quadrilateral with two distinct pairs of congruent consecutive sides (but not all sides congruent).
Trapezoid		A quadrilateral with *exactly* one pair of parallel sides.

The following shows the relationships between the different kinds of quadrilaterals.

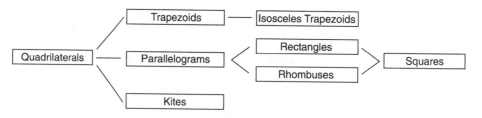

The table below shows the properties of the different types of parallelograms.

PROPERTIES	PARALLELO-GRAM	RECTANGLE	RHOMBUS	SQUARE
Opposite sides are parallel.	X	X	X	X
Opposite sides are congruent.	X	X	X	X
Opposite angles are congruent.	X	X	X	X
The diagonals bisect each other.	X	X	X	X
Consecutive angles are supplementary.	X	X	X	X
All angles are congruent.		X		X
The diagonals are congruent.		X		X
All sides are congruent.			X	X
The diagonals bisect the angles.			X	X
The diagonals are perpendicular.			X	X

Here are additional properties for the quadrilaterals that are not classified as parallelograms:

Kites

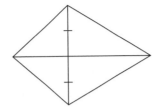

- Exactly one of the diagonals is the perpendicular bisector of the other diagonal.

Isosceles Trapezoids

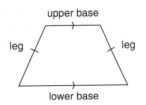

- The two legs are congruent.
- The bases are parallel.
- The lower base angles are congruent.
- The upper base angles are congruent.
- The diagonals are congruent.
- Any lower base angle is the supplement of any upper base angle.

Model Problem 1   Given: $\square ABCD$ with m$\angle B = 70°$.

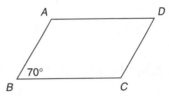

Find the measures of $\angle C$, $\angle D$, and $\angle A$.

Solution   Step 1.   m$\angle D$ = m$\angle B$ = 70°, because the opposite angles of a parallelogram are congruent. (Similarly, m$\angle C$ = m$\angle A$.)

Step 2.   m$\angle B$ + m$\angle A$ = 180, because any pair of consecutive angles in a parallelogram are supplementary.

$$m\angle B + m\angle A = 180$$
$$70 + m\angle A = 180$$
$$m\angle A = 110°$$

Thus, m$\angle C$ = m$\angle A$ = 110°.
Therefore, if m$\angle B$ = 70°, then m$\angle D$ = 70°, m$\angle A$ = 110°, and m$\angle C$ = 110°.

Model Problem 2   Given: $\square COAT$ with m$\angle A = x$ and m$\angle T = (3x - 8)$.

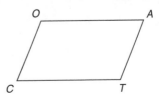

Find the measures of $\angle A$ and $\angle T$.

Solution   m∠A + m∠T = 180, because any pair of consecutive angles in a parallelogram are supplementary.

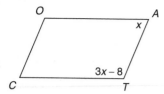

$$m\angle A + m\angle T = 180$$
$$x + 3x - 8 = 180$$
$$4x - 8 = 180$$
$$4x = 188$$
$$x = 47$$

Therefore, m∠A = x = 47° and m∠T = 3x − 8 = 3(47) − 8 = 133°.

Model Problem 3   Given square $ABCD$, find the length of side $\overline{AB}$.

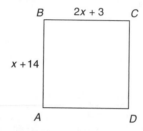

Solution   In a square, all the sides are congruent. Thus,

$$AB = BC$$
$$x + 14 = 2x + 3$$
$$14 = x + 3$$
$$11 = x$$

Therefore, $AB = x + 14 = 11 + 14 = 25$.

Model Problem 4   **Given:** Rhombus $WXYZ$ with diagonal $\overline{ZX}$.

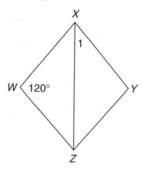

Find the measure of ∠1.

Solution   Step 1.   m∠WXY = 60° since consecutive angles are supplementary.

Step 2.   m∠1 = $\frac{1}{2}$ m∠WXY since the diagonals of a rhombus bisect its angles.

Therefore, m∠1 = $\frac{1}{2}$(60) = 30°.

Model Problem 5   Given: ▱WXYZ.

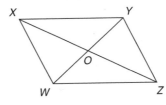

Justify each of the following statements.

a $\overline{WX} \parallel \overline{ZY}$

b $XO = \frac{1}{2}(XZ)$

c $XY = WZ$

d $\angle XWZ \cong \angle XYZ$

Solution   **a** Opposite sides of a parallelogram are parallel.
b The diagonals of a parallelogram bisect each other.
c Opposite sides of a parallelogram are congruent.
d Opposite angles of a parallelogram are congruent.

Model Problem 6   A trapezoid and its median are shown below.

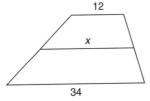

Find the length of the median, x.

> **Note:** The **median** of a trapezoid is the line segment which joins the midpoints of the legs, with the length of the median given by the following formula:
>
> $$median = \frac{1}{2}(upper\ base + lower\ base)$$

Solution

$$median = \frac{1}{2}(upper\ base + lower\ base)$$

$$x = \frac{1}{2}(34 + 12)$$

$$x = \frac{1}{2}(46)$$

$$x = 23$$

Therefore, the length of the median is 23 units.

TRY THESE

1. In ▱ABCD, m∠A = 75°.

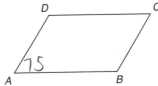

Find the measures of ∠D, ∠C, and ∠B.

2. In □COAT, CA = 18 centimeters.

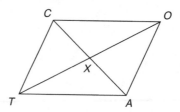

Find CX.

3. List the properties of the diagonals of a rectangle.

 4. In isosceles trapezoid *HIJK*, m∠I = 120°.

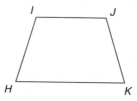

Find the measures of ∠K, ∠J, and ∠H.

5. Given rhombus *PTRA*, find the measures of ∠R, ∠A, ∠1, and ∠2.

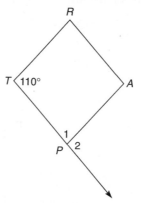

6. When is a square also a rectangle? Explain.

7. What is the name of a quadrilateral with four congruent sides and four congruent angles?

8. **Given:** Rectangle *ABCD* with *AE* = 12.

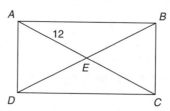

Find *DB*.

9. A quadrilateral with exactly one pair of parallel sides is called a ? .

1. In □COAT, m∠C = 85°.

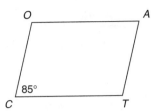

What is the measure of ∠O?

A 85°

B 90°

C 95°

D 175°

2. **Given:** □GHJK with m∠2 = 59° and m∠4 = 42°.

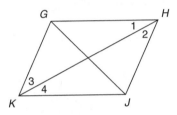

The measure of ∠GHJ is ? .

F 42°

G 59°

H 79°

J 101°

3. In □ABCD, AD = 20 feet.

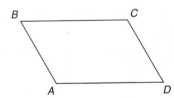

What is the length of $\overline{BC}$?

A 40 feet

B 20 feet

C 15 feet

D 10 feet

4. **Given:** Trapezoid WXYZ with median $\overline{MN}$.

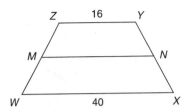

What is the length of $\overline{MN}$?

F 56

G 46

H 28

J 20

5. Which is a property of rectangles?

A The angles are not congruent.

B The diagonals are congruent and bisect each other.

C The diagonals are not congruent.

D The sides are congruent.

6. **Given:** □BOAT with m∠B = 88°.

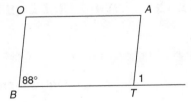

What is the measure of ∠1?

F 92°

G 88°

H 78°

J 62°

7. **Given:** Trapezoid *ABCD* with median $\overline{MN}$.

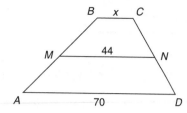

What is the value of *x*?

A 95

B 57

C 26

D 18

8. If the diagonals of a quadrilateral are congruent, then the quadrilateral must be a __?__ .

F parallelogram

G rectangle

H rhombus

J trapezoid

9. If a quadrilateral is a kite, then —

A two pairs of consecutive sides are congruent.

B four pairs of consecutive sides are congruent.

C one of the angles measures 90°.

D opposite sides are parallel.

10. Figure *KMNO* is a rectangle with *MX* = 15 cm.

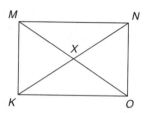

What is the length of $\overline{KN}$?

F 7.5 cm

G 10 cm

H 15 cm

J 30 cm

PRACTICE 15   Proving That a Quadrilateral Is a Specific Type of Quadrilateral

Objective:	SOL G.8.b

❏ The student will prove the properties of quadrilaterals using algebraic and coordinate methods as well as deductive reasoning.

Proving a Quadrilateral a Parallelogram

Let's start by looking at the properties that are used to classify a quadrilateral as a parallelogram.

A Quadrilateral Is a Parallelogram When
- Both pairs of opposite sides are parallel, OR
- Both pairs of opposite sides are congruent, OR
- One pair of opposite sides is both parallel and congruent, OR
- Both pairs of opposite angles are congruent, OR
- The diagonals bisect each other, OR
- Consecutive angles are supplementary.

Model Problem 1 Given: Quadrilateral $ABCD$ with $A(0, 0)$, $B(4, 7)$, $C(8, 7)$, and $D(4, 0)$.

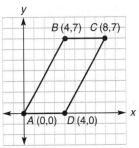

Prove that $ABCD$ is a parallelogram by showing that
a the diagonals bisect each other, OR
b both pairs of opposite sides are congruent.

Solution for a The midpoint of a line is the point that bisects the line. Thus, if the midpoints of the diagonals $\overline{AC}$ and $\overline{DB}$ are located at the same point, then they bisect each other. Find the midpoints of $\overline{AC}$ and $\overline{DB}$. The formula for the midpoint is $\left(\dfrac{x_1 + x_2}{2}, \dfrac{y_1 + y_2}{2}\right)$.

MIDPOINT OF $\overline{AC}$	**MIDPOINT OF $\overline{DB}$**
Let $(x_1, y_1) = A(0, 0)$ and $(x_2, y_2) = C(8, 7)$.	Let $(x_1, y_1) = D(4, 0)$ and $(x_2, y_2) = B(4, 7)$.
midpoint of $\overline{AC} = \left(\dfrac{0 + 8}{2}, \dfrac{0 + 7}{2}\right)$	midpoint of $\overline{DB} = \left(\dfrac{4 + 4}{2}, \dfrac{0 + 7}{2}\right)$
midpoint of $\overline{AC} = \left(\dfrac{8}{2}, \dfrac{7}{2}\right) = \left(4, 3\frac{1}{2}\right)$	midpoint of $\overline{DB} = \left(\dfrac{8}{2}, \dfrac{7}{2}\right) = \left(4, 3\frac{1}{2}\right)$

Since the midpoints of $\overline{AC}$ and $\overline{DB}$ are located at the same point, $\left(4, 3\frac{1}{2}\right)$, $\overline{AC}$ and $\overline{DB}$ bisect each other. Therefore, since the diagonals bisect each other, quadrilateral $ABCD$ is a parallelogram.

Solution for b Use the distance formula, $D = \sqrt{(x_2 - x_1)^2 + (y_2 - y_1)^2}$, to show that opposite sides are congruent. First, prove $\overline{AB} \cong \overline{CD}$.

LENGTH OF $\overline{AB}$	**LENGTH OF $\overline{CD}$**
Let $(x_1, y_1) = A(0, 0)$ and $(x_2, y_2) = B(4, 7)$.	Let $(x_1, y_1) = C(8, 7)$ and $(x_2, y_2) = D(4, 0)$.
$AB = \sqrt{(4 - 0)^2 + (7 - 0)^2}$	$CD = \sqrt{(4 - 8)^2 + (0 - 7)^2}$
$AB = \sqrt{(4)^2 + (7)^2} = \sqrt{65}$	$CD = \sqrt{(^-4)^2 + (7)^2} = \sqrt{65}$

Thus, $\overline{AB} \cong \overline{CD}$. Next, show that the other pair of opposite sides ($\overline{BC}$ and $\overline{AD}$), are congruent.

LENGTH OF $\overline{BC}$	**LENGTH OF $\overline{AD}$**
Let $(x_1, y_1) = B(4, 7)$ and $(x_2, y_2) = C(8, 7)$.	Let $(x_1, y_1) = A(0, 0)$ and $(x_2, y_2) = D(4, 0)$.
$BC = \sqrt{(8 - 4)^2 + (7 - 7)^2}$	$AD = \sqrt{(4 - 0)^2 + (0 - 0)^2}$
$BC = \sqrt{(4)^2 + (0)^2} = \sqrt{16} = 4$	$AD = \sqrt{(4)^2 + (0)^2} = \sqrt{16} = 4$

Thus, $\overline{BC} \cong \overline{AD}$. Therefore, since both pairs of opposite sides are congruent, quadrilateral $ABCD$ is a parallelogram.

Once it is known that a quadrilateral is a parallelogram, there are certain properties that can be used to show that the parallelogram is a rectangle, a rhombus, or a square.

A Parallelogram Is a Rectangle When

• At least one angle is a right angle, OR

• The diagonals are congruent.

A Parallelogram Is a Rhombus When

• At least one pair of consecutive sides is congruent, OR

• At least one diagonal bisects a pair of opposite angles, OR

• The diagonals are perpendicular to each other.

A Parallelogram Is a Square When

• It is both a rectangle and a rhombus.

REMEMBER

To prove that a *quadrilateral* is a rhombus, show that the diagonals are perpendicular bisectors of each other.

Model Problem 2   **Given:** $\square ABCD$ with $A(^-2, 1)$, $B(2, 4)$, $C(5, 0)$, and $D(1, ^-3)$.

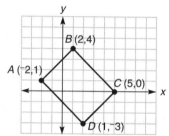

Prove that $ABCD$ is a square.

Solution   To prove that $ABCD$ is a square, we need to show that it is both a rhombus and a rectangle.

Step 1.   Show that $ABCD$ is a rhombus. A parallelogram is a rhombus if it has a pair of congruent consecutive sides. Check $\overline{AB} \cong \overline{BC}$ (any two consecutive sides will do).

LENGTH OF $\overline{AB}$	LENGTH OF $\overline{BC}$
Let $(x_1, y_1) = A(^-2, 1)$ and $(x_2, y_2) = B(2, 4)$.	Let $(x_1, y_1) = B(2, 4)$ and $(x_2, y_2) = C(5, 0)$.
$AB = \sqrt{(2 - {}^-2)^2 + (4 - 1)^2}$	$BC = \sqrt{(5 - 2)^2 + (0 - 4)^2}$
$AB = \sqrt{(4)^2 + (3)^2}$	$BC = \sqrt{(3)^2 + (^-4)^2}$
$AB = \sqrt{16 + 9} = \sqrt{25}$	$BC = \sqrt{9 + 16} = \sqrt{25}$
$AB = 5$	$BC = 5$

Thus, $\overline{AB} \cong \overline{BC}$, and so $ABCD$ is a rhombus.

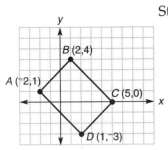

Step 2. Show that $ABCD$ is a rectangle. A parallelogram is a rectangle if it has a right angle. A right angle is formed when two consecutive sides are perpendicular; this means that their slopes are negative reciprocals of each other. Check $\overline{AB} \perp \overline{BC}$ (any two consecutive sides will do) by using the slope formula, $m = \dfrac{y_2 - y_1}{x_2 - x_1}$.

SLOPE OF $\overline{AB}$	SLOPE OF $\overline{BC}$
Let $(x_1, y_1) = A(^-2, 1)$ and $(x_2, y_2) = B(2, 4)$.	Let $(x_1, y_1) = B(2, 4)$ and $(x_2, y_2) = C(5, 0)$.
slope of $\overline{AB} = \dfrac{4 - 1}{2 - ^-2} = \dfrac{3}{2 + 2} = \dfrac{3}{4}$	slope of $\overline{BC} = \dfrac{0 - 4}{5 - 2} = \dfrac{^-4}{3}$

Since the slopes of $\overline{AB}$ and $\overline{BC}$ are negative reciprocals of each other, $\overline{AB} \perp \overline{BC}$ or $\angle ABC$ is a right angle. This proves that $ABCD$ is a rectangle. Therefore, since $ABCD$ is both a rectangle and a rhombus, it is also a square.

Model Problem 3 Given: $\overline{SH} \cong \overline{OP}$, $\angle 1 \cong \angle 2$, and $m\angle 2 = 90°$.

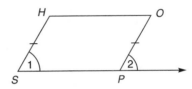

Prove that quadrilateral $SHOP$ is a rectangle.

Solution First show that $SHOP$ is a parallelogram.

STATEMENTS	REASONS
1. $\overline{SH} \parallel \overline{OP}$	1. $\angle 1$ and $\angle 2$ are congruent corresponding angles.
2. $\overline{SH} \cong \overline{OP}$	2. Given.
3. $SHOP$ is a parallelogram.	3. A pair of opposite sides is both congruent and parallel.

Once you have shown that $SHOP$ is a parallelogram, prove that it is also a rectangle.

STATEMENTS	REASONS
1. $m\angle 1 = m\angle 2 = 90°$	1. Given.
2. $SHOP$ is a rectangle.	2. $SHOP$ is a parallelogram with a right angle.

A Trapezoid Is Isosceles When
- The legs are congruent, OR
- The diagonals are congruent, OR
- The upper base angles are congruent, OR
- The lower base angles are congruent.

A Quadrilateral Is a Kite When
- Exactly two non-overlapping pairs of consecutive sides are congruent, OR
- Exactly one diagonal is the perpendicular bisector of the other diagonal.

Model Problem 4   Prove that quadrilateral $ABCD$ is an isosceles trapezoid.

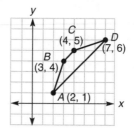

Solution   In the figure, $\overline{BC}$ appears to be parallel to $\overline{AD}$. Check to see if this conjecture is true.

$$\text{slope of } \overline{BC} = \frac{5-4}{4-3} = 1$$

$$\text{slope of } \overline{AD} = \frac{6-1}{7-2} = \frac{5}{5} = 1$$

The conjecture is true. Thus, $ABCD$ is a trapezoid. If $ABCD$ is also isosceles, then its legs must be congruent. Check $\overline{AB} \cong \overline{DC}$.

$$AB = \sqrt{(3-2)^2 + (4-1)^2} = \sqrt{(1)^2 + (3)^2} = \sqrt{1+9} = \sqrt{10}$$

$$DC = \sqrt{(7-4)^2 + (6-5)^2} = \sqrt{(3)^2 + (1)^2} = \sqrt{9+1} = \sqrt{10}$$

Thus, the legs are congruent. Therefore, $ABCD$ is an isosceles trapezoid.

TRY THESE

1.   **Given:** Quadrilateral $WXYZ$ with $\overline{WX} \cong \overline{ZY}$ and $\angle 1 \cong \angle 2$.

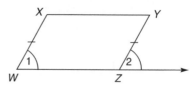

Prove that $WXYZ$ is a parallelogram.

2. **Given:** Quadrilateral $ABCD$ with $A(1, 3)$, $B(3, 9)$, $C(9, 10)$, and $D(7, 4)$.

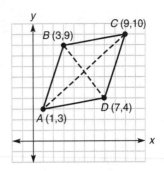

Show that the diagonals $\overline{BD}$ and $\overline{AC}$ bisect each other.

3. Prove that quadrilateral $GEOM$ is a parallelogram.

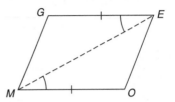

4. **Given:** $\square ABCD$.

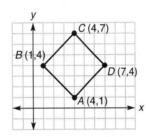

Prove that $\square ABCD$ is a rhombus.

5. **Given:** $\square POXY$ with $\angle POY \cong \angle XOY$ and $\angle PYO \cong \angle XYO$.

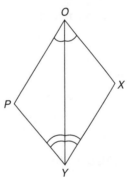

Prove that $\square POXY$ is a rhombus.

6. Given rectangle $CITY$ with $C(0, 0)$, $I(0, 5)$, $T(7, 5)$, and $Y(7, 0)$, prove that the diagonals of $CITY$ are congruent.

7. **Given:** Quadrilateral $ABCD$ with $\angle A \cong \angle C$ and $\angle D \cong \angle B$.

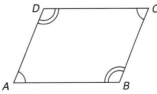

Why is $ABCD$ a parallelogram?

1. Which can be used to prove that a parallelogram is a rhombus?

   A The diagonals are congruent.

   B The diagonals are perpendicular.

   C The diagonals bisect each other.

   D The diagonals bisect each other and are congruent.

2. **Given:** □*ABCD* with *A*(4, 2), *B*(2, 5), *C*(5, 7), and *D*(7, 4).

   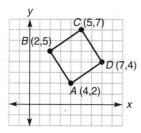

   Why is □*ABCD* a rectangle?

   F The slopes of the sides are all equal.

   G The slopes of opposite sides are equal.

   H The slopes of one pair of opposite sides are negative reciprocals.

   J The slopes of one pair of consecutive sides are negative reciprocals.

3. Which does *not* prove that a quadrilateral is a parallelogram?

   A The diagonals bisect each other.

   B Both pairs of opposite sides are congruent.

   C One pair of opposite sides is parallel.

   D One pair of opposite sides is parallel and congruent.

4. **Given:** Quadrilateral *ABCD* with $\overline{AE} \cong \overline{EC}$ and $\overline{DE} \cong \overline{EB}$.

   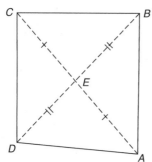

   ABCD is a ? .

5. **F** rhombus

   G rectangle

   H parallelogram

   J trapezoid

5. Which can be used to prove that a parallelogram is a square?

   A All sides are congruent.

   B All angles are right angles.

   C One pair of consecutive sides is congruent and perpendicular.

   D The diagonals are congruent.

6. **Given:** Quadrilateral *ABCD* with $\overline{AD} \parallel \overline{BC}$ and $\overline{AB} \cong \overline{BC}$.

   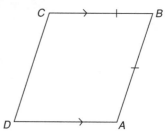

   Can you conclude that *ABCD* is a parallelogram?

   F No, only one pair of sides must be parallel.

   G No, the same pair of opposite sides must be congruent and parallel.

   H Yes, one pair of opposite sides is parallel.

   J Yes, one pair of opposite sides is parallel and the other pair is congruent.

7. **Given:** Quadrilateral *ABCD* with $\overline{AB} \parallel \overline{CD}$.

   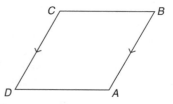

   Which of the following must be true in order for *ABCD* to be a parallelogram?

   A $\overline{AD} \cong \overline{BC}$

   B $\overline{AD} \parallel \overline{BC}$

   C $\angle A \cong \angle B$

   D $\angle C \cong \angle D$

8. Which can be used to prove that a trapezoid is isosceles?

    F Consecutive angles are supplementary.

    G Exactly one pair of opposite sides is parallel.

    H Opposite angles are congruent.

    J The diagonals are congruent.

9. **Given:** Quadrilateral *WXYZ* with $\overline{WX} \cong \overline{XY}$.

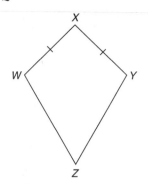

Which of the following must be true in order for *WXYZ* to be a kite?

    A $\angle X \cong \angle Z$

    B $\overline{WZ} \cong \overline{WX}$ and $\overline{XY} \cong \overline{YZ}$

    C $\overline{WZ} \cong \overline{YZ}$

    D $\overline{WZ} \cong \overline{YZ}$ and $\overline{WZ} \not\cong \overline{WX}$

10. **Given:** Quadrilateral *RSTU*.

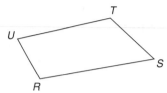

If $\overline{UT}$ is parallel to $\overline{RS}$ and $\overline{UR}$ is parallel to $\overline{ST}$, then *RSTU* must be a __?__ .

    F trapezoid

    G rectangle

    H rhombus

    J parallelogram

PRACTICE 16   Applications with Quadrilaterals

Objective:	SOL G.8.c

    ❐ **The student will use properties of quadrilaterals to solve practical problems.**

Quadrilaterals can be seen in building and furniture designs, in art, and in many other areas of life. For example, most sports playing fields are rectangular-shaped. Architects use parallelograms when drawing blueprints. Quadrilaterals are used in many quilt designs and art deco pictures.

Model Problem 1   Mr. Brown wants to build a rectangular foundation from three pieces of wood that are 15, 17, and 28 feet long. The longest piece is the exact length of the diagonal, while the two shorter pieces will be joined to form the other diagonal.

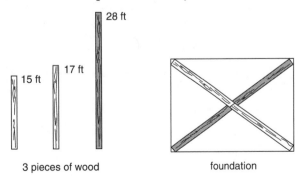

3 pieces of wood   foundation

How long must Mr. Brown cut the two shorter pieces if they are to be equal in length?

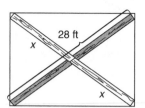

Solution The diagonals of a rectangle are congruent. Thus, the diagonal formed by the two shorter pieces must be 28 feet long. Let x represent the length of the shorter pieces. Then

$$x + x = \text{length of the diagonal}$$
$$2x = 28$$
$$x = 14$$

Therefore, both pieces must be cut to a length of 14 feet.

Model Problem 2 Given: $\square MNOP$ with diagonals $\overline{OM}$ and $\overline{NP}$, m$\angle 1 = 35°$, and m$\angle 3 = 48°$.

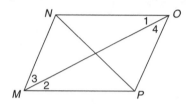

Find the measure of $\angle NMP$.

Solution $\overline{NO}$ is parallel to $\overline{MP}$, because opposite sides of a parallelogram are parallel. With $\overline{OM}$ as the transversal, $\angle 1$ and $\angle 2$ are a pair of congruent alternate interior angles. Thus, m$\angle 1 = $ m$\angle 2 = 35°$, and

$$\text{m}\angle NMP = \text{m}\angle 2 + \text{m}\angle 3$$

Substitute m$\angle 2 = 35°$ and m$\angle 3 = 48°$.

$$\text{m}\angle NMP = 35° + 48°$$
$$\text{m}\angle NMP = 83°$$

Areas of Quadrilaterals **Area** is the amount of space that a figure occupies. **Perimeter** is the distance around a figure. The table below lists the area and perimeter for different types of quadrilaterals.

> **Note:** Area is usually represented by the symbol A, and perimeter is usually represented by the symbol P.

QUADRILATERAL	AREA	PERIMETER
Parallelogram 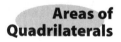	$A = bh$	$P = 2s_1 + 2s_2$ s_1 and s_2 are the lengths of the sides.
Rectangle	$A = bh$ (or $A = \ell w$)	$P = 2s_1 + 2s_2$ s_1 and s_2 are the lengths of the sides.

(continued)

QUADRILATERAL	AREA	PERIMETER
Rhombus 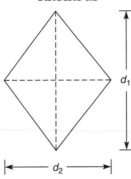	$A = \frac{1}{2} d_1 d_2$	$P = 2s_1 + 2s_2$ s_1 and s_2 are the lengths of the sides.
Square  s	$A = s^2$	$P = 4s$
Trapezoid 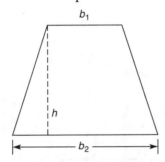	$A = \frac{1}{2}(b_1 + b_2)h$	$P = s_1 + s_2 + s_3 + s_4$ s_1, s_2, s_3 and s_4 are the lengths of the sides.

Model Problem 3 Scott wants to build a frame for his graduation photo. If the area of the picture is 140 cm² and its width is 4 cm longer than its length, what are the dimensions of the picture?

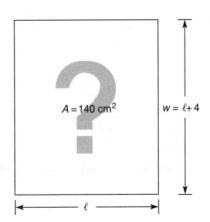

Solution First, find the length (ℓ) by using the area formula, $A = \ell w$. We are given $A = 140$ cm^2 and $w = \ell + 4$. Substitute these values into the formula, and solve for ℓ.

$$\ell w = A$$
$$(\ell)(\ell + 4) = 140$$
$$\ell^2 + 4\ell = 140$$
$$\ell^2 + 4\ell - 140 = 0$$
$$(\ell - 10)(\ell + 14) = 0$$
$$\ell - 10 = 0 \text{ or } \ell + 14 = 0$$
$$\ell = 10 \text{ or } \ell = {}^-14$$

$\ell = {}^-14$ cannot be used (since there are no negative lengths); therefore $\ell = 10$. Next, use the length, $\ell = 10$, and the formula, $w = \ell + 4$, to find the width (w).

$$w = \ell + 4 = 10 + 4 = 14$$

Therefore, the width is 14 cm and the length is 10 cm.

TRY THESE

1. The spindles on the railing of the porch form a trapezoid. If the center spindle corresponds to the median of the trapezoid, find the length of the center spindle, x.

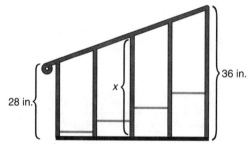

2. **Given:** Square *RSVT*.

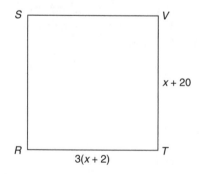

    Find the area of *RSVT*.

3. How many meters of wire fencing are needed to enclose the rectangular garden in the figure below?

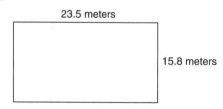

4. Given: $\square WXYZ$ with $\angle YZA = 80°$.

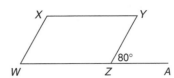

Find the measure of $\angle X$.

5. If the figure below is an isosceles trapezoid, what is the value of x?

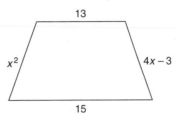

ASSESSMENT

1. How much material is needed to cover the top of the box if each side measures 5 cm?

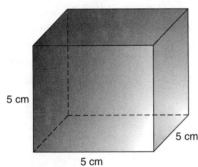

A 20 cm^2

B 25 cm^2

C 125 cm^2

D 150 cm^2

2. A window is constructed from nine different panels. If each panel measures 8 inches by 9 inches, what is the area of the window, ignoring the seams?

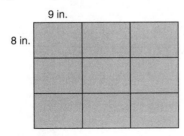

F 72 sq in.

G 442 sq in.

H 576 sq in.

J 648 sq in.

3. Given: Trapezoid $FGHI$.

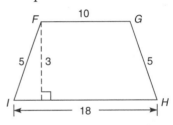

Find the area of the trapezoid.

A 38 square units

B 42 square units

C 70 square units

D 84 square units

4. Edward wishes to carpet his rectangular patio, whose dimensions are 30 feet by 27 feet. How much will it cost Edward to cover the patio if the carpet costs $3.95 per square yard?

F $1,066.50

G $533.25

H $450.30

J $355.50

5. Given: $\square ADCB$ with $AB = (3x + 13)$ and $DC = (7x - 3)$.

Find the value of x.

A 4

B 2.5

C 1.6

D 1

6. Leanne recognized that the side-view of a lampshade takes the shape of an isosceles trapezoid. If the bases are 24 and 35 inches long and the perimeter is 103 inches, what are the lengths of the legs?

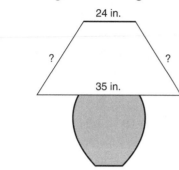

24 in.

? ?

35 in.

F 22 inches

G 28 inches

H 44 inches

J 46 inches

For problems 7 and 8 use ▱MNOP given in the figure below.

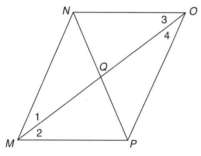

7. If $NP = 24$, then $NQ = $ _?_ .

A 48

B 24

C 16

D 12

8. If $m\angle 1 = 42°$ and $m\angle 2 = 37°$, then $m\angle NOP = $ _?_ .

F 37°

G 42°

H 79°

J 101°

9. Suppose that the ratio of $m\angle W$ to $m\angle X$ in ▱WXYZ is 2:3. What are the measures of the angles in WXYZ?

Hint: If two quantities A and B are in the ratio a:b, then $A = a \cdot n$ and $B = b \cdot n$, where n is the common factor to be solved for.

A $\angle W = 32°$, $\angle X = 48°$, $\angle Y = 32°$, $\angle Z = 48°$

B $\angle W = 32°$, $\angle X = 48°$, $\angle Y = 40°$, $\angle Z = 60°$

C $\angle W = 72°$, $\angle X = 108°$, $\angle Y = 72°$, $\angle Z = 108°$

D $\angle W = 72°$, $\angle X = 108°$, $\angle Y = 108°$, $\angle Z = 72°$

10. Hugo wishes to paint the four walls of a room. The dimensions of each wall are 10 meters by 6 meters. If each square meter of wall costs $0.24 to paint, how much will it cost Hugo to paint the four walls?

F $7.68

G $14.40

H $30.72

J $57.60

PRACTICE 17   Interior and Exterior Angles of Polygons

Objective: **SOL G.9**

❑ The student will use measures of interior and exterior angles of polygons to solve problems. Tessellations and tiling problems will be used to make connections to art, construction, and nature.

Polygons   A **polygon** is a closed figure in a plane formed by three or more line segments (called **sides**) such that

1. Each side intersects exactly two other sides, one at each endpoint (called **vertices**).

2. No two intersecting sides are **collinear,** that is, no two intersecting sides form a straight line.

Examples of Polygons

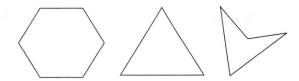

Examples of Non-polygons

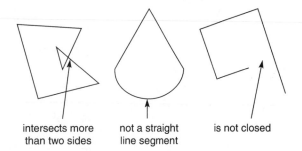

intersects more
than two sides

not a straight
line segment

is not closed

   Some polygons are named according to the number of sides (or the number of interior angles) that they have. Often, if there is no name given to a polygon, the name *n*-**gon** is used, where *n* is the number of sides (or angles). The table below lists the various types of polygons.

NAME OF POLYGON	NUMBER OF SIDES (NUMBER OF ANGLES)	EXAMPLES
Triangle	3	
Quadrilateral	4	
Pentagon	5	
Hexagon	6	

(*continued*)

NAME OF POLYGON	NUMBER OF SIDES (NUMBER OF ANGLES)	EXAMPLES
Heptagon	7	
Octagon	8	
Nonagon	9	
Decagon	10	
Dodecagon	12	
Pentadecagon	15	
n-gon	n	

Every polygon is either convex or concave. A polygon is **concave** when one of its interior angles measures more than 180°.

Examples of Concave Polygons

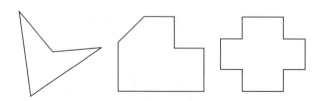

For the remainder of this practice, unless stated otherwise, polygons will be assumed to be convex.

A polygon is **convex** when it is not concave, that is, when all of its interior angles measure less than 180°.

Examples of Convex Polygons

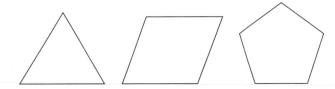

Angles of Polygons

An **exterior** angle is an angle formed by extending a side at a vertex. There are always two exterior angles at each vertex, and each exterior angle forms a linear pair with the interior angle at the *same* vertex.

Example

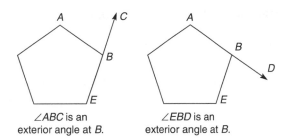

∠ABC is an exterior angle at B.   ∠EBD is an exterior angle at B.

The sum of the measures of the exterior angles (taking one exterior angle at each vertex) does not depend on the type of polygon and is always equal to 360°.

The Sum of the Measures of the Exterior Angles

For any polygon, the sum of the measures of the exterior angles, taking one exterior angle at each vertex, is 360°.

On the other hand, the sum of the measures of the interior angles *does* depend on the type of polygon (or on the number of sides). Recall from Practice 1 that the formula is given by the following:

The Sum of the Measures of the Interior Angles

The sum of the measures of the interior angles of a polygon is

$$(n - 2)180°$$

where n is the number of sides (or interior angles).

This formula comes from dividing the interior of the polygon into non-overlapping triangles and taking the sum of the measures of the angles of the triangles. For example, a pentagon can be divided into three triangles by drawing all of the diagonals at a single vertex.

(continued)

Interior and Exterior Angles of Polygons • 113

In general, any *n*-sided polygon can be divided into (*n* − 2) triangles by this method. Since the sum of the angles of a triangle is 180°, we can obtain the sum of the interior angles of a pentagon by multiplying 180° by the number of triangles formed, or 3 · 180° = 540°.

Model Problem 1   For each polygon below, find the sum of the measures of (1) the interior angles and (2) the exterior angles.

    a A pentagon

    b A 35-sided polygon

Solution	SUM OF THE INTERIOR ANGLES	SUM OF THE EXTERIOR ANGLES
a Let *n* = 5. (5 − 2)180° = (3)180° = 540°		360°
b b Let *n* = 35. (35 − 2)180° = (33)180° = 5,940°		360°

Model Problem 2   Find the measure of one interior angle of a regular hexagon.

Solution 1   A hexagon is a six-sided figure. The interior angle sum is (6 − 2)180° = (4)180° = 720°. The polygon is also regular, so the interior angles are all congruent. Therefore, each interior angle measures 720° ÷ 6 = 120°.

REMEMBER

Polygons can be equiangular and equilateral. If a polygon is both equilateral and equiangular, it is called a **regular** polygon.

Solution 2   This problem can be solved by finding the measure of one exterior angle and then using the fact that one exterior and one interior angle are supplementary (one exterior angle + one interior angle = 180°).

    The sum of the measures of the exterior angles is 360°. Since there are six congruent exterior angles, each exterior angle measures 360° ÷ 6 = 60°.

$$\text{one exterior angle} + \text{one interior angle} = 180°$$
$$60° + \text{one interior angle} = 180°$$
$$\text{one interior angle} = 120°$$

Therefore, one interior angle measures 120°.

Model Problem 3

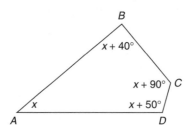

What are the measures of the interior angles?

Solution   The polygon has four sides, so the sum of the measures of the interior angles is (4 − 2)180° = (2)180° = 360°. Solve for *x*.

$$m\angle A + m\angle B + m\angle C + m\angle D = 360.$$
$$x + (x + 40) + (x + 90) + (x + 50) = 360$$
$$4x + 180 = 360$$
$$4x = 180$$
$$x = 45$$

Therefore,

$$m\angle A = x = 45°$$

$$m\angle B = x + 40 = 45° + 40° = 85°$$

$$m\angle C = x + 90 = 45° + 90° = 135°$$

$$m\angle D = x + 50 = 45° + 50° = 95°$$

The following box lists formulas and relationships that are true for regular polygons *only*.

When Working With *Regular* Polygons

- One exterior angle + one interior angle = 180°.
- The measure of one exterior angle = 360° ÷ n.
- The measure of one interior angle = 180° − one exterior angle.
- The number of sides (n) = 360° ÷ one exterior angle

The box below summarizes the formulas and relationships that are true for *any* polygon.

When Working With *Any* Polygon

- The sum of the measures of the interior angles = $(n - 2)180°$.
- The sum of the measures of the exterior angles = 360°.
- One exterior angle + one interior angle = 180°
  (but only for exterior and interior angles located at the same vertex).
- The number of sides (n) = $\dfrac{\text{sum of the interior angles}}{180°} + 2$.

Model Problem 4   The sum of the measures of the interior angles of a regular polygon is 1,440°. How many sides does this polygon have?

Solution 1   Using the "number of sides" formula,

$$n = \frac{\text{sum of the interior angles}}{180°} + 2$$

$$= \frac{1{,}440°}{180°} + 2$$

$$= 8 + 2$$

$$= 10$$

Therefore, this polygon has ten sides.

(continued)

Solution 2 The sum of the measures of the interior angles is $(n - 2)180° = 1,440°$. Find a value for n (the number of sides) that solves this equation.

$$(n - 2)180° = 1,440°$$

$$n - 2 = \frac{1,440°}{180°}$$

$$n - 2 = 8$$

$$n = 10$$

Therefore, this polygon has ten sides.

Tessellations and Tilings A **tessellation** (or a **tiling**) is an arrangement of non-overlapping polygons covering the entire plane without leaving gaps. Tessellations using only one type of polygon are called **pure tessellations**; pure tessellations using only congruent *regular* polygons are called **regular tessellations**.

Examples of Pure and Regular Tessellations

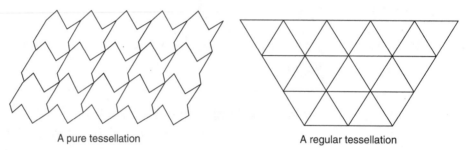

A pure tessellation   A regular tessellation

Tessellations involving two or more types of regular polygons are called **semi-regular tessellations**.

Examples of Semi-Regular Tessellations

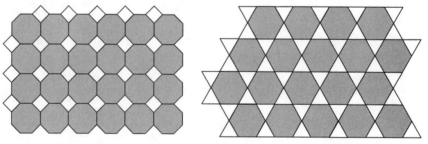

Two semi-regular tessellations

Model Problem 5 The face of a honeycomb consists of interlocking regular hexagons.

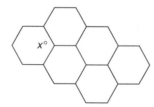

Find the value of x.

Solution   A regular hexagon has six congruent angles and sides, so the sum of the interior angles equals $(6 - 2)180° = 720°$. The interior angles of a regular polygon are all congruent. Therefore, to find the measure of an interior angle, divide 6 into $720°$. The measure of an interior angle $= 720 ÷ 6 = 120°$ or $x = 120°$.

TRY THESE

1. For each polygon, find the sum of the measures of the interior angles.
   a A hexagon
   b A dodecagon
   c A 20-sided polygon

2. For each polygon, find the measure of one interior angle.
   a A STOP sign
   b A regular decagon

3. Find the measures of the interior angles of the polygon below.

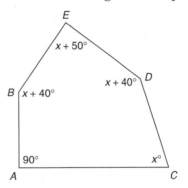

4. Each of the exterior angles of a certain regular polygon measures 72°. How many sides does this polygon have?

5. The following tiling is made with regular triangles.

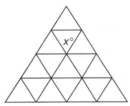

   Find the value of x.

ASSESSMENT

1. The sum of the measures of the interior angles of a heptagon is —
   A 360°
   B 900°
   C 1,080°
   D 1,260°

2. Given the following figure, find the value of x.

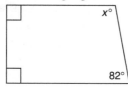

F 82°

G 90°

H 98°

J 108°

3. Each exterior angle of a regular polygon measures 45°. How many sides does this polygon have?

A 4 sides

B 5 sides

C 6 sides

D 8 sides

4. The sum of the interior angles of a polygon is 4,320°. How many sides does this polygon have?

F 12 sides

G 14 sides

H 24 sides

J 26 sides

5. Given the following polygon, find the value of x.

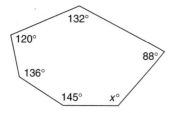

A 92°

B 97°

C 99°

D 120°

6. What is the sum of the measures of the exterior angles of a pentagon (taking one exterior angle at each vertex)?

F 720°

G 540°

H 360°

J 180°

7. The figure below shows an interior angle of a regular polygon. How many sides does this polygon have?

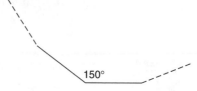

A 12 sides

B 14 sides

C 20 sides

D 30 sides

8. What is the measure of one interior angle of a regular 24-sided polygon?

F 90°

G 108°

H 164°

J 165°

9. Find the value of x in the polygon below.

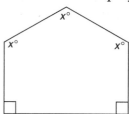

A 60°

B 72°

C 108°

D 120°

10. The following is a semi-regular tessellation using octagons and squares.

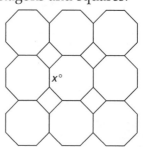

What is the value of x?

F 108°

G 120°

H 135°

J 150°

PRACTICE 18 Circles

Objective:	SOL G.10

☐ The student will investigate and solve practical problems involving circles, using properties of angles, arcs, chords, tangents, and secants. Problems will include finding arc length and area of a sector and may be drawn from applications of architecture, art, and construction.

Chords, Tangents, and Secants

A **circle** is the set of points in a plane that are equidistant from a fixed point, called the **center** of the circle. In symbols, a circle with center P is denoted by $\odot P$.

TERM	DEFINITION	EXAMPLE
Radius	A segment joining the center of a circle to a point on the circle.	
Diameter	A segment passing through the center of a circle with its endpoints on the circle.	$\overline{AP}$ and $\overline{PB}$ are radii. $\overline{AB}$ is a diameter.
Circumference	The perimeter of a circle—the distance around the circle.	

The table below shows the basic definitions involving chords, secants, and tangents.

TERM	DEFINITION	EXAMPLE
Chord	A segment whose endpoints are on a circle.	
Secant	A line intersecting a circle at exactly two points.	$\overline{AB}$ is a chord. Line s is a secant.
Tangent	A line intersecting a circle at exactly one point.	
Point of Tangency	The point on a circle where a tangent line intersects the circle.	Line t is a tangent. D is the point of tangency.
Tangent Circles	Two circles intersecting each other at exactly one point.	

If a line is tangent to a circle, then it is perpendicular to the line containing the center of the circle and the point of tangency. For example,

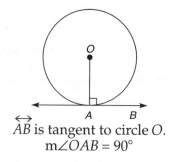

$\overleftrightarrow{AB}$ is tangent to circle O.
$m\angle OAB = 90°$

Model Problem 1 **Given:** Circle O with tangent $\overline{ZW}$.

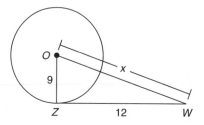

Find the value of x.

Solution Since $\overline{ZW}$ is tangent to circle O, it is perpendicular to $\overline{OZ}$. Thus, we have a right triangle with a missing hypotenuse.

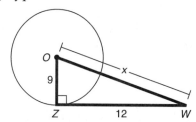

Use the formula $a^2 + b^2 = c^2$, with $a = 9$, $b = 12$, and $c = x$, and solve for x.

$$a^2 + b^2 = c^2$$
$$9^2 + 12^2 = x^2$$
$$81 + 144 = x^2$$
$$225 = x^2$$
$$\sqrt{225} = x$$
$$15 = x$$

Therefore, $x = 15$ units.

Segments formed by Intersecting Chords, Secants, and Tangents

TYPE OF SEGMENTS	DEFINITION AND FORMULA	EXAMPLE
Chord-Chord	Segments formed by two chords intersecting inside of a circle. *The product of the segments of one chord = the product of the segments of the other.*	$(AO)(OC) = (DO)(OB)$
Secant-Secant	Segments formed by two secants intersecting outside of a circle. *The product of one secant segment and its external part = the product of the other secant segment and its external part.*	$(FH)(GH) = (IH)(JH)$
Tangent-Secant	Segments formed by a tangent and a secant intersecting outside of a circle. *The square of the tangent segment = the product of the secant segment and its external part.*	$(TV)^2 = (SV)(OV)$
Tangent-Tangent	Segments formed by two tangents intersecting outside of a circle. *The length of one tangent segment = the length of the other tangent segment.*	$AP = BP$

Model Problem 2 For each circle, find the value of x.

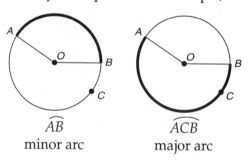

Circle I   Circle II   Circle III

Solution **Circle I** Type of segments: *chord-chord*
Formula: *The product of the segments of one chord = the product of the segments of the other chord.*

$$2x = (4)(10)$$
$$2x = 40$$
$$x = 20$$

Circle II Type of segments: *secant-secant*
Formula: *The product of one secant segment and its external part = the product of the other secant segment and its external part.*

$$(12)(5) = (15)(x)$$
$$60 = 15x$$
$$4 = x$$

Circle III Type of segments: *secant-tangent*
Formula: *The square of the tangent segment = the product of the secant segment and its external part.*

$$x^2 = (12 + 4)(4) = (16)(4) = 64$$
$$x = \sqrt{64} = 8$$

Arcs and Angles An **arc** consists of two points on a circle and all the points on the circle between them. The smaller arc is called the **minor arc**; the larger arc is called the **major arc** and is usually named by three points. For example,

$\overarc{AB}$ $\overarc{ACB}$

minor arc   major arc

TERM	DEFINITION AND FORMULA	EXAMPLE
Central Angle	An angle whose vertex is the center of the circle. *The measure of a central angle = the measure of the intercepted arc.*	 $m\angle 1 = m\widehat{AB}$
Inscribed Angle	An angle formed by two chords whose vertex is on the circle. *The measure of an inscribed angle = one-half the measure of the intercepted arc.*	 $m\angle 2 = \frac{1}{2} m\widehat{AB}$

Note: A **semicircle** is any arc measuring 180°.

Model Problem 3   Find the measures of angles 1 and 2 in the circles below.

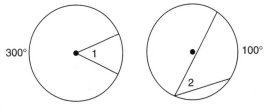

Solution   ∠1   Type of angle: *central*
Formula: *The measure of a central angle equals the measure of the intercepted arc.*
The measure of the intercepting arc is 360° − 300° or 60°. Thus, m∠1 = 60°.

∠2   Type of angle: *inscribed*
Formula: *The measure of an inscribed angle equals one-half the measure of the intercepted arc.*

$$m\angle 2 = \frac{1}{2}(100°) = 50°$$

TYPE OF ANGLE	DEFINITION AND FORMULA	EXAMPLE
Chord-Chord	An angle formed by two chords intersecting inside of a circle. *The measure of a chord-chord angle = one-half the sum of the arcs intercepted by the angle and its vertical angle.*	$m\angle 1 = \frac{1}{2}\left(m\widehat{AC} + m\widehat{BD}\right)$
Chord-Tangent	An angle formed by a chord and a tangent. *The measure of a chord-tangent angle = one-half the measure of the intercepted arc.*	$m\angle 2 = \frac{1}{2}m\widehat{ACB}$
Secant-Secant	An angle formed by two secants intersecting outside of a circle. *The measure of a secant-secant angle = one-half the difference of the measures of the intercepted arcs.*	$m\angle 3 = \frac{1}{2}\left(m\widehat{AC} - m\widehat{BD}\right)$
Secant-Tangent	An angle formed by a secant and a tangent intersecting outside of a circle. *The measure of a secant-tangent angle = one-half the difference of the measures of the intercepted arcs.*	$m\angle 4 = \frac{1}{2}\left(m\widehat{AC} - m\widehat{BC}\right)$
Tangent-Tangent	An angle formed by two tangents intersecting outside of a circle. *The measure of a tangent-tangent angle = one-half the difference of the measures of the intercepted arcs.*	$m\angle 5 = \frac{1}{2}\left(m\widehat{ACB} - m\widehat{AB}\right)$

Model Problem 4

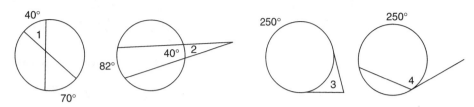

Find the measures of angles 1 to 4.

Solution   ∠1   Type of angle: *chord-chord*

$$m\angle 1 = \frac{1}{2} \text{ (the sum of the arcs intercepted by the angle and its vertical angle)}$$

$$m\angle 1 = \frac{1}{2}(40° + 70°) = \frac{1}{2}(110°)$$

$$m\angle 1 = 55°$$

∠2   Type of angle: *secant-secant*

$$m\angle 2 = \frac{1}{2} \text{ (the difference of the measures of the intercepted arcs)}$$

$$m\angle 2 = \frac{1}{2}(82° - 40°) = \frac{1}{2}(42°)$$

$$m\angle 2 = 21°$$

∠3   Type of angle: *tangent-tangent*
The missing intercepting arc measures 360° − 250° or 110°. Thus,

$$m\angle 3 = \frac{1}{2} \text{ (the difference of the measures of the intercepted arcs)}$$

$$m\angle 3 = \frac{1}{2}(250° - 110°) = \frac{1}{2}(140°)$$

$$m\angle 3 = 70°$$

∠4   Type of angle: *chord-tangent*

$$m\angle 4 = \frac{1}{2} \text{ (the measure of the intercepted arc)}$$

$$m\angle 4 = \frac{1}{2}(250°) = 175°$$

Model Problem 5   If $m\angle 1 = 60°$ and $m\widehat{AB} = 80°$, find the measure of $\widehat{CD}$.

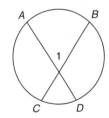

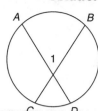

Solution We are given m∠1 = 60° and m$\widehat{AB}$ = 80°. Angle 1 is a chord-chord angle; its measure equals one-half the sum of the measures of the arcs intercepted by the angle and its vertical angle.

$$m\angle 1 = \frac{1}{2}(m\widehat{AB} + m\widehat{CD})$$

Substitute m∠1 = 60° and m$\widehat{AB}$ = 80°. Solve for the measure of $\widehat{CD}$.

$$60° = \frac{1}{2}(80° + m\widehat{CD})$$
$$120° = 80° + m\widehat{CD}$$
$$40° = m\widehat{CD}$$

Therefore, m$\widehat{CD}$ = 40°.

Arcs and Chords

Relationship Between Arcs and Chords in a Circle or in Congruent Circles

- Congruent chords have congruent arcs.
- Congruent arcs have congruent chords.
- Congruent chords are equidistant from the center.
- Chords equidistant from the center are congruent.
- A diameter perpendicular to a chord bisects the chord and its intercepting arcs.

Model Problem 6 Find the length of $\overline{HG}$ in the circles below.

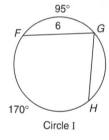
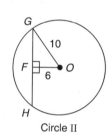

Circle I   Circle II

Solution **Circle I** m$\widehat{FG}$ = 95°

m$\widehat{HF}$ = 170°

m$\widehat{HF}$ + m$\widehat{FG}$ = 265°

Thus, the measure of the missing arc ($\widehat{HG}$) is 360° − 265° = 95°, and so arc $\widehat{FG}$ is congruent to arc $\widehat{HG}$. If two arcs in the same circle are congruent, then their chords are congruent. Therefore, if $\overline{FG}$ = 6, then $\overline{HG}$ = 6.

Circle II Triangle *GFO* is a right triangle. Use the formula $a^2 + b^2 = c^2$, with $a = FG$, $b = 6$, and $c = 10$ and solve for *FG*.

$$(FG)^2 + 6^2 = 10^2$$
$$(FG)^2 + 36 = 100$$
$$(FG)^2 = 64$$
$$FG = 8$$

$FH = FG = 8$, because a diameter that is perpendicular to a chord bisects the chord. ($\overline{OF}$ is part of a diameter.) Therefore, $HG = FG + FH = 16$.

Area of a Sector and Arc Length

A **sector** of a circle is a region bounded by two radii and an arc of the circle. For example,

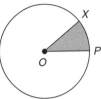

The shaded region represents sector XOP.

REMEMBER

Area of circle $= \pi r^2$

Circumference of a circle $= 2\pi r$

The formula for the area of a sector uses the formula for the area of a circle and arc length uses the circumference formula.

Area of a Sector

If n represents the arc measure and r represents the radius of the circle, then

$$\text{Area of the sector} = \frac{n}{360°} \cdot \pi r^2$$

Arc Length

If n represents the arc measure and r represents the radius of the circle, then

$$\text{Arc length} = \frac{n}{360°} \cdot 2\pi r$$

Model Problem 7

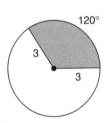

a   Find the area and circumference of the circle.

b   Find the area of the shaded sector and the length of the arc.

Solution   a   Use the formula for area $A = \pi r^2$ with $r = 3$.

$$A = \pi(3)^2 = 9\pi$$

Note: Unless you are given a value for π, do not calculate π. In geometry, π is usually approximated by either 3.14 or $\frac{22}{7}$.

Use the formula for circumference $C = 2\pi r$ with $r = 3$.

$$C = 2\pi(3) = 6\pi$$

b Use the formula for the area of a sector $\frac{n}{360°} \cdot \pi r^2$ with $n = 120°$ and $r = 3$.

$$\text{Area of the sector} = \frac{120°}{360°} \cdot \pi (3)^2$$

$$\text{Area of the sector} = \frac{1}{3} \cdot 9\pi$$

$$\text{Area of the sector} = 3\pi$$

Use the formula for arc length $\frac{n}{360°} \cdot 2\pi r$ with $n = 120°$ and $r = 3$.

$$\text{Arc length} = \frac{120°}{360°} \cdot 2\pi \cdot 3$$

$$\text{Arc length} = \frac{1}{3} \cdot 6\pi$$

$$\text{Arc length} = 2\pi$$

Note: You need to learn the formulas dealing with the circle because many of these formulas are not on the formula sheet for geometry.

TRY THESE

1. Find the measures of angles 1 to 3 in the circles below.

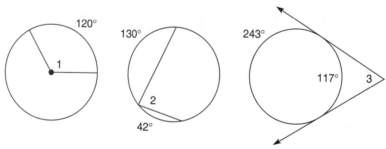

2. What is the value of x?

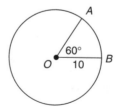

3. **Given:** m∠*AOB* = 60° and *OB* = 10.

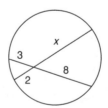

Find the area of sector *AOB*.

4. Two chords are located 5 inches from the center of a circle.

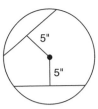

What is true about the two chords?

5. A circle with radius 12 has a central angle ∠XWY measuring 45°.

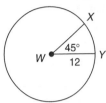

Find the length of arc $\widehat{XY}$.

6. The radius of ⊙P is 15 centimeters. A tangent segment to the circle, $\overline{CD}$, is 20 centimeters long. Find the length of $\overline{PD}$.

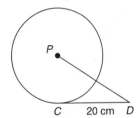

7. The area of a circle is 121π. Find the radius of the circle.

ASSESSMENT

1.

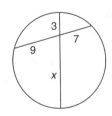

What is the value of x?

A 5

B 5.33

C 21

D 48

2. **Given:** ⊙O with tangent segment $\overline{DT}$, $\overline{DT}$ = 6 feet, and $\overline{AT}$ = 4 feet.

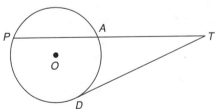

Find $\overline{PT}$.

F 5 ft

G 9 ft

H 20 ft

J 32 ft

3. Find the length of arc $\overset{\frown}{XY}$.

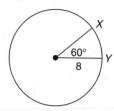

A 2π

B 4π

C 8π

D 16π

4. Find the measure of $\overset{\frown}{XW}$.

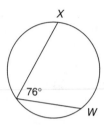

F $284°$

G $152°$

H $76°$

J $38°$

5. **Given:** $m\overset{\frown}{TO} = 165°$, $m\overset{\frown}{RP} = 85°$, and $m\overset{\frown}{PO} = 75°$.

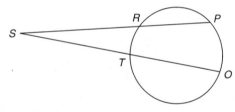

Find $m\angle S$.

A $75°$

B $55°$

C $35°$

D $20°$

6. **Given:** Tangents $\overrightarrow{PT}$ and $\overrightarrow{PQ}$ with points of tangency T and Q, respectively.

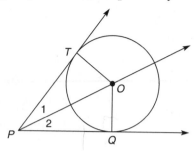

If $m\angle 1 = 30°$, find $m\angle 2$.

F $15°$

G $30°$

H $45°$

J $60°$

7.

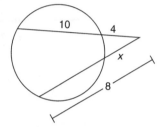

What is the value of x?

A 3.2

B 5

C 7

D 17.5

8. If a pizza pie with a diameter of 12 inches is cut into eight equal slices, what is the area of one slice?

F 1.5π sq in.

G 3π sq in.

H 4.5π sq in.

J 18π sq in.

9. If the circumference of a circle is 87.92 feet, what is the radius of the circle?

A 5.3 ft

B 7 ft

C 14 ft

D 28 ft

10. A circle is inscribed in a triangle. All the segments are tangent to the circle. Find the value of x.

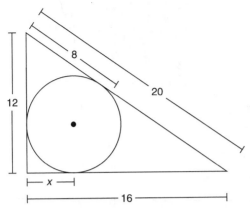

F 8

G 6

H 4

J 2

11. Given $\odot O$ with a radius of 8 inches and $\angle AOB = 90°$.

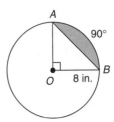

Use $\pi = 3.14$ and find the area of the shaded region.

A 2.28 inches

B 18.24 inches

C 34.24 inches

D 68.48 inches

PRACTICE 19   Cumulative Practice on SOLs G.8a–c, 9, and 10

1. *KMNO* is a rectangle with $\overline{MO} = 36$ centimeters.

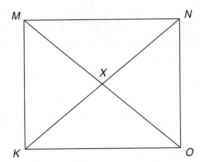

The length of *MX* is ____ .

A 72 cm

B 36 cm

C 24 cm

D 18 cm

2. Given: $\square ABCD$, $AD = (4x + 20)$, and $BC = (3x + 27)$.

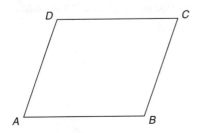

What is the value of x?

F 1

G 6.7

H 7

J 47

3. In the figure below, what is the measure of $\angle 3$?

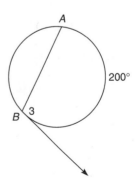

A 200°

B 180°

C 160°

D 100°

4. Which is a method of proving that a quadrilateral is a parallelogram?

    F One pair of opposite sides is parallel.

    G One pair of opposite sides is congruent.

    H The diagonals do not bisect each other.

    J One pair of opposite sides is congruent and parallel.

5. The sum of the measure of the interior angles of an 11-gon is __?__

    A 360°

    B 880°

    C 1,620°

    D 1,800°

6. Which can be used to prove that a quadrilateral is a parallelogram?

    F If the slopes of consecutive sides are equal, then the quadrilateral is a parallelogram.

    G If the slopes of opposite sides are equal, then the quadrilateral is a parallelogram.

    H If the slopes of opposite sides are not equal, then the quadrilateral is a parallelogram.

    J If the slopes of the sides are all equal, then the quadrilateral is a parallelogram.

7. **Given:** $\odot P$ with tangent segment $\overline{CD}$.

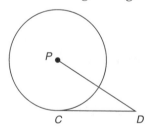

If $CD = 24$ inches and $PD = 25$ inches, then the radius = __?__

    A 1 inch

    B 7 inches

    C 35.7 inches

    D 49 inches

8. The following figure is a cube-shaped box with sides of length 5 centimeters. How much material is needed to cover the box?

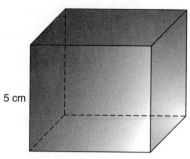

5 cm

    F 100 cm²

    G 125 cm²

    H 150 cm²

    J 500 cm²

9. **Given:** $\square GHJK$ with m∠2 = 33° and m∠4 = 51°.

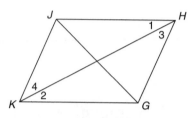

What is the measure of ∠KJH?

    A 96°

    B 84°

    C 51°

    D 33°

10. The measure of an exterior angle of a regular polygon is 36°. How many sides does the polygon have?

    F 10

    G 8

    H 7

    I 5

11. **Given:** Trapezoid *GHIJ*.

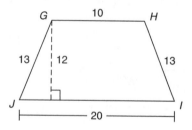

What is the area of the trapezoid?

    A 180 units²

    B 195 units²

    C 220 units²

    D 364 units²

12. Given: Trapezoid *ABCD* with median $\overline{MN}$.

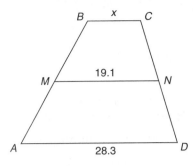

What is the value of *x*?

F 9.2

G 9.9

H 23.7

J 37.5

13. The sum of the exterior angles of a convex polygon with 25 sides is —

A 4,500°

B 4,140°

C 720°

D 360°

14. Given: Quadrilateral *ABCD* with $\overline{AD} \parallel \overline{BC}$ and $\overline{AB} \cong \overline{BC}$.

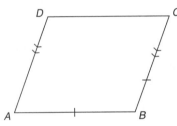

Do you have enough information to conclude that *ABCD* is a parallelogram?

F No, *ABCD* could be a trapezoid.

G No, consecutive sides are not parallel.

H Yes, one pair of consecutive sides is congruent.

J Yes, one pair of opposite sides is parallel.

15. Given: $m\widehat{AB} = 88°$ and $m\widehat{CD} = 32°$.

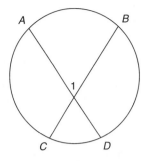

What is the measure of $\angle 1$?

A 120°

B 60°

C 56°

D 28°

16. A walkway 2 meters wide surrounds a rectangular play area 50 meters long and 30 meters wide. Find the area of the walkway.

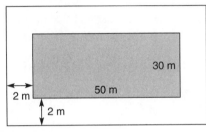

F 336 m²

G 268 m²

H 228 m²

J 100 m²

17. If the diagonals of a parallelogram are perpendicular, then the parallelogram is a —

A kite

B trapezoid

C rhombus

D rectangle

18. The picture below shows an interior angle of a regular polygon. How many sides does this polygon have?

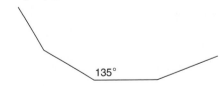

F 8 sides

G 16 sides

H 24 sides

J 32 sides

19. Which can be used to show that a parallelogram is a square?

   A If the diagonals bisect the angles of the parallelogram, then the parallelogram is a square.

   B If the diagonals of the parallelogram are congruent, then the parallelogram is a square.

   C If the diagonals of the parallelogram are not congruent, then the parallelogram is a square.

   D If the parallelogram has a pair of congruent consecutive sides and a right angle, then the parallelogram is a square.

20.

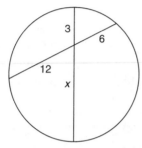

In the figure above, the value of x is —

   F 6

   G 12

   H 24

   J 36

21. **Given:** Rhombus $PTRA$ with $PT = (3x - 1)$ and $PA = (x + 7)$.

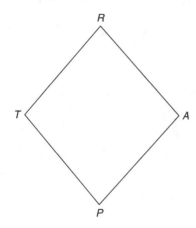

What is the perimeter of the rhombus?

   A 48

   B 44

   C 16

   D 9

22 Which is *not* a property of rectangles?

   F Both pairs of opposite sides are parallel.

   G The angles are right angles.

   H The diagonals are congruent.

   J The diagonals bisect the angles.

23. **Given:** $m\overarc{AB} = 200°$ and $m\overarc{AC} = 68°$.

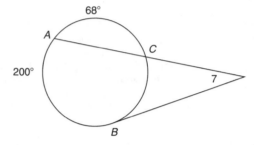

What is the measure of $\angle 7$?

   A 54°

   B 66°

   C 108°

   D 146°

24. What is the measure of one interior angle of a regular 16-gon?

   F 11.25°

   G 22.5°

   H 157.5°

   J 168.75°

25. Which is *not* a property of rhombi?

   A The diagonals are congruent.

   B The diagonals are perpendicular.

   C Opposite sides are congruent.

   D Opposite sides are parallel.

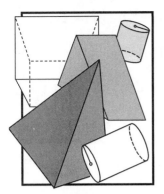

UNIT 4
Three-Dimensional Figures

PRACTICE 20   Three-Dimensional Objects

Objective:	SOL G.12

❐ The student will make a model of a three-dimensional figure from a two-dimensional drawing and make a two-dimensional representation of a three-dimensional object. Models and representations will include scale drawings, perspective drawings, blueprints, or computer simulations.

Three-Dimensional Figures & Nets

Up to this point, the geometric figures presented have all been two-dimensional with length and width only. We are now at a point where it is necessary to study three-dimensional objects, which have length, width, and height.

Some three-dimensional figures have both flat and curved surfaces. For example, **cylinders** consist of two congruent circular bases and a main region, and **cones** consist of one base and a curved surface.

Examples of Cylinders

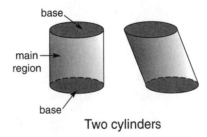

Two cylinders

Examples of Cones

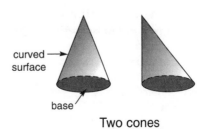

Two cones

Another group of three-dimensional figures are called **polyhedrons**; this type of three-dimensional figure consists of flat surfaces bounded by polygons, or **faces**. The lines where the faces intersect are called **edges**. The corners of the polygons making up the faces are called the **vertices** of the polyhedron.

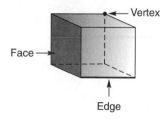

Prisms and pyramids are two examples of polyhedrons. A **prism** has two congruent parallel faces (called **bases**), and the other faces (called **lateral faces**) are all parallelograms.

Examples of Prisms

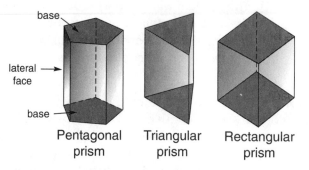

Pentagonal prism   Triangular prism   Rectangular prism

A **pyramid** is a polyhedron with a single polygonal base and a set of triangles meeting at a single point (called the **apex**).

Examples of Pyramids

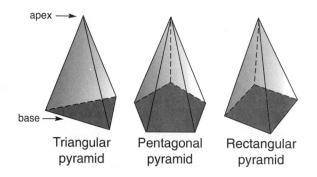

Triangular pyramid   Pentagonal pyramid   Rectangular pyramid

These definitions are helpful when constructing a three-dimensional figure from a **net** (a two-dimensional pattern that can be folded into a three-dimensional solid).

Model Problem 1 Draw a net for the three-dimensional figure below.

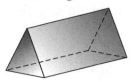

Solution The figure is a triangular prism with triangles for the bases and rectangles for the lateral faces.

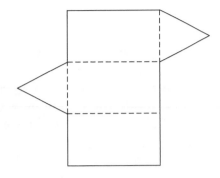

Model Problem 2 Identify the three-dimensional figure formed by folding this net.

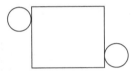

Solution The figure has two congruent circular regions and a main region. Therefore the figure is a cylinder.

Scale Models The second part of this practice deals with real world objects and representing them in scale drawings, perspective drawings, and blueprints. In scale drawings and blueprints, real world objects are drawn to a scale (called the **scale factor**) representing the ratio between the size of the model and the true size of the object. In perspective drawings, objects are drawn in such a way that they look the same as they appear to the eye. Please note that in a perspective drawing part of the object cannot be seen because it is hidden from the eye.

Model Problem 3 A scale model of a car is 5.5 inches high. The scale factor is 1 to 11. Find the height of the car.

Solution The ratio is 1:11, which means that 1 inch of the model = 11 inches of the car. Let x = the actual height of the car, write a proportion, and solve for x.

$$\frac{1}{11} = \frac{5.5}{x}$$
$$x = (11)(5.5)$$
$$x = 60.5 \text{ inches}$$

Therefore the height of the car is 60.5 inches.

Viewing Three-Dimensional Objects

The last concept discussed in this practice will be to identify a three-dimensional solid from different points of view such as the front, side, or top.

Model Problem 4   Draw the top view of this three-dimensional figure.

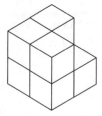

Solution   The top view shows three squares on the first level plus one square on the second level. The square on the second level will have a dark line segment indicating a break in the surface.

TRY THESE

1. Draw the net for a square pyramid.

2. The distance between two cities on a map is $2\frac{1}{2}$ inches. The scale key indicates that $\frac{1}{4}$ of an inch equals 50 miles. What is the actual distance between the two cities?

3. The net below represents which three-dimensional solid?

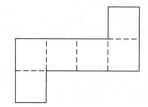

4. John needs to make a scale drawing of his 20 feet by 16 feet living room floor on a piece of paper. What are the dimensions of the scale drawing if John wants $\frac{1}{8}$ of an inch to equal 2 feet?

5. The faces of two buildings are parallel to you. How many vanishing points (points of perspective) does the picture show?

6. On a map, 1 centimeter represents 25 miles. Two cities 355 miles apart would be how many centimeters apart on the map?

7. In the scale drawing below, x represents the actual length of the garage.

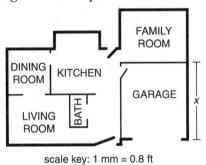

scale key: 1 mm = 0.8 ft

The length of the garage (x) = _?_ .

 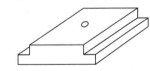 ASSESSMENT

1. Use the drawing below and determine which represents the top view.

A   B   C 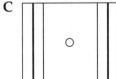   D

2. The following pattern can be folded into a —

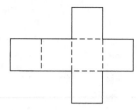

   F cube

   G cylinder

   H square

   J triangular pyramid

3. Which represents the front view of this three-dimensional object?

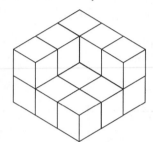

   A

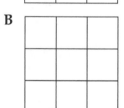

   B

   C

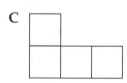

   D

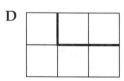

4. Carl needs to make a model of a cube that will be $\frac{1}{8}$ of its actual size. One edge of the cube is 55 inches. What is the length of one edge of the scale model?

   F $6\frac{7}{8}$ in.

   G 6 in.

   H 7 in.

   J $7\frac{7}{8}$ in.

5. Identify the top view of this three-dimensional object.

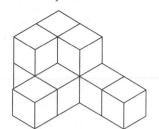

   A

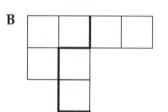

   B

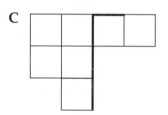

   C

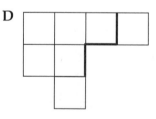

   D

6. Which is the net of a cone?

   F

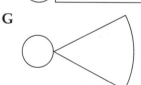

   G

   H

J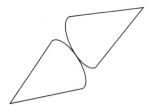

H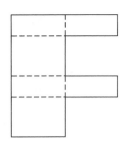

7. The class assignment is to make a scale model of a cube with edges that are 160 feet long.

160'

160'   160'

If $\frac{1}{4}$ inch = 5 feet, what will be the length of one edge of the scale model?

A 32 in.

B 16 in.

C 8 in.

D 4 in.

8. Which is a net for the right rectangular prism below?

F

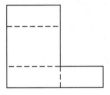

G

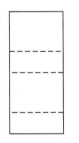

J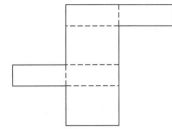

9. A scale model of a birthday cake is 2" by 4" by 1".

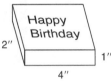

Happy Birthday

2"

1"

4"

If $\frac{1}{8}$ inch = 1 inch (of the actual size), what are the true dimensions of the cake?

A 4" by 8" by 1"

B 16" by 20" by 4"

C 16" by 32" by 8"

D 20" by 32" by 8"

10. The net below is a _____?_____.

F Triangular pyramid

G Triangular prism

H Square pyramid

J Rectangular prism

PRACTICE 21   Surface Area and Volume of Three-Dimensional Objects

Objective:	SOL G.13

❏ **The student will use formulas for surface area and volume of three-dimensional objects to solve practical problems. Calculators will be used to find the decimal approximation for results.**

In this practice, two main concepts will be studied: finding the surface area and volume of cylinders, prisms, pyramids, cones, and spheres. A formula sheet with appropriate formulas is provided during the test, along with a calculator so that a decimal approximation can be determined. The table below contains these formulas.

Note: Throughout this practice, B = area of the base and p = perimeter of the base.

TYPE OF OBJECT	FORMULA FOR SURFACE AREA	FORMULA FOR VOLUME
Cone	$S.A. = \pi r(\ell + r)$	$V = \frac{1}{3}\pi r^2 h$
Cylinder	$S.A. = 2\pi r(h + r)$	$V = \pi r^2 h$
Rectangular Prism	$S.A. = 2(\ell w + \ell h + wh)$	$V = \ell wh$
Prism	$S.A. = hp + 2B$	$V = Bh$
Pyramid	$S.A. = \frac{1}{2}\ell p + B$	$V = \frac{1}{3}Bh$
Sphere	$A = 4\pi r^2$	$V = \frac{4}{3}\pi r^3$

Model Problem 1   A can of dog food has a diameter of 1.6 inches and a height of 4.5 inches. What is the surface area of the can to the nearest tenth of an inch? Use $\pi = 3.14$.

Solution   The can takes the shape of a cylinder.

4.5 in.

⊢1.6 in.⊣

To find the surface area, use the formula: $S.A. = 2\pi r(h + r)$.

$$\pi = 3.14$$
$$h = 4.5 \text{ in.}$$
$$r = \frac{1}{2} \text{ (diameter)} = \frac{1}{2} (1.6) = 0.8 \text{ in.}$$

Substitute the given values into the formula.

$$S.A. = 2\pi r(h + r)$$
$$S.A. = 2(3.14)(0.8)(4.5 + 0.8)$$
$$S.A. = (5.024 \text{ in.})(5.3 \text{ in.})$$
$$S.A. = 26.6272 \text{ sq in.}$$
$$S.A. \approx 26.6 \text{ sq in.}$$

TI KEYSTROKES

ON 2 2nd ^ .8 (4.5 + .8) ENTER

Answer: 26.2 sq in.

CASIO KEYSTROKES

AC/ON 1 2 SHIFT EXP × .8

(4.5 + .8) EXE

Answer: 26.2 sq in.

Note: When you enter π into the calculator instead of 3.14, you will get a slightly different answer. Thus, you will need to pick the answer choice that is *closest* to your answer. If no match can be made, redo your calculations using 3.14.

Model Problem 2   A jawbreaker (a piece of candy) has a diameter of 2 centimeters. Find the volume of the jawbreaker to the nearest tenth of a centimeter. Use $\pi = 3.14$.

Solution   The jawbreaker takes the shape of a sphere.

⊢— 2 cm —⊣

$$\pi = 3.14$$

$$r = \frac{1}{2} \text{ (of the diameter)} = \frac{1}{2} (2 \text{ cm}) = 1 \text{ cm}$$

Substitute the given values into the formula for volume.

$$V = \frac{4}{3}\pi r^3$$

$$V = \frac{4}{3}(3.14)(1 \text{ cm})^3 = 4.187$$

$$V \approx 4.2 \text{ cm}^3$$

(continued)

ON (4 ÷ 3) 2nd ^ 1 ^ 3 ENTER   AC/ON 1 4 ÷ 3 × SHIFT EXP × 1
                                                            ^ 3 EXE

The answer is 4.2 cm³.   The answer is 4.2 cm³.

Model Problem 3 How much wrapping paper is needed to wrap the package shown below?

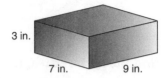

Solution The solid is a prism with $\ell = 9$ inches, $w = 7$ inches, and $h = 3$ inches.
The formula for finding the surface area of a prism is $S.A. = 2(\ell w + \ell h + wh)$.
Substitute the given values into the formula.

$$S.A. = 2(9 \cdot 7 + 9 \cdot 3 + 7 \cdot 3)$$
$$S.A. = 2(63 + 27 + 21)$$
$$S.A. = 2(111)$$
$$S.A. = 222 \text{ sq in.}$$

Model Problem 4 Find the volume of the right trapezoidal prism below.

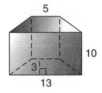

Solution $V = Bh$

B = the area of the base (the trapezoid)

h = the height of the prism (the distance between the two bases)

First find the area of the base. From the formula sheet, the formula for the area
of a trapezoid is $A = \frac{1}{2}h(b_1 + b_2)$. Note that the h in this formula is the height
of the base figure and not the height of the prism.

$$h = 3$$
$$b_1 = 13$$
$$b_2 = 5$$

Substitute these values into the area formula for trapezoids.

$$A = \tfrac{1}{2}(3)(13 + 5)$$
$$A = \tfrac{1}{2}(3)(18)$$
$$A = \tfrac{1}{2}(54)$$
$$A = 27 \text{ square units}$$

Therefore, $B = 27$ square units.

Now substitute the values for B and h into the formula $V = Bh$.

$$B = 27$$
$$h = 10$$
$$V = (27)(10)$$
$$V = 270 \text{ cubic units}$$

Model Problem 5   One side of the base of a square pyramid is 16 feet long. If the height of the pyramid is 15 feet, what is its surface area?

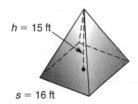

$h = 15$ ft

$s = 16$ ft

Solution   The formula for the surface area of a pyramid is $S.A. = \frac{1}{2}\ell p + B$.

You are given the height ($h = 15$ feet) and the length of one side of the square base ($s = 16$ feet). However, the slant height (ℓ), the perimeter of the base (p), and the area of the base (B) are needed to find the surface area.

The area of the square base (B) $= s^2 = 16^2 = 256$ sq ft.
The perimeter of the square base (p) $= 4s = 4 \cdot 16 = 64$ ft.

To find the slant height, notice that a right triangle is formed by the height (h), half the length of one side $\left(\frac{1}{2}s\right)$, and the slant height ($\ell$).

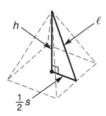

h ℓ

$\frac{1}{2}s$

Use the Pythagorean Theorem $a^2 + b^2 = c^2$, with $a = h = 15$, $b = \frac{1}{2}s = 8$, and $c = \ell$, to solve for the slant height (ℓ).

$$15^2 + 8^2 = \ell^2$$
$$225 + 64 = \ell^2$$
$$289 = \ell^2$$
$$\sqrt{289} = \ell^2$$
$$17 = \ell$$

Substitute the values for the slant height, perimeter, and area into the formula for the surface area.

$$S.A. = \frac{1}{2}(17 \text{ ft})(64 \text{ ft}) + 256 \text{ ft}^2 = \frac{1}{2}(1088 \text{ ft}^2) + 256 \text{ ft}^2 = 800 \text{ ft}^2$$

Therefore, the surface area of the pyramid is 800 square feet.

1. Find the volume of the solid below.

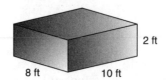

2 ft

8 ft   10 ft

2. Find the surface area of a cone with a height of 4 centimeters and a radius of 3 centimeters, to the nearest centimeter. Use π = 3.14.

3. Find the volume of the solid below.

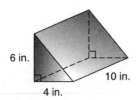

6 in.

10 in.

4 in.

4. A barn silo consists of a cylinder with a hemisphere on top.

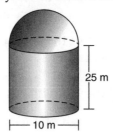

25 m

10 m

Find the surface area of the silo. Leave the answer in terms of π.

5. Find the volume of the unshaded solid. Use π = 3.14.

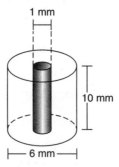

1 mm

10 mm

6 mm

ASSESSMENT

1. The base of a square pyramid has an area of 144 square feet.

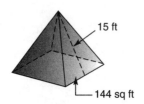

15 ft

144 sq ft

If the slant height of the pyramid is 15 feet, then its surface area is __?__.

A 360 sq ft
B 504 sq ft
C 1,080 sq ft
D 1,224 sq ft

2. A cylindrical container has a diameter of 3.5 inches and a height of 2.8 inches.

The volume of the container to the nearest tenth of an inch is __?__.

F 26.9 cu in.

G 30.8 cu in.

H 43.1 cu in.

J 107.8 cu in.

3. One side of a cube measures 7 meters. What is the surface area of the cube?

Hint: A cube is a prism with square bases.

A 392 m²

B 343 m²

C 294 m²

D 196 m²

4. The water level of a cylindrical tank with a diameter of 10 inches is 6 inches high. When Aaron submerged a rock in the tank, the water level went up to 6.6 inches. What is the volume of the rock, to the nearest inch?

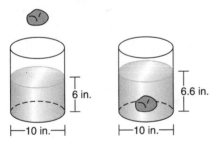

F 47 cu in.

G 59 cu in.

H 62 cu in.

J 87 cu in.

5. A box in the shape of a rectangular prism (4 inches by 6 inches by 1.2 inches) contains three pieces of chalk.

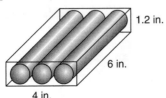

Each piece of chalk takes the shape of a cylinder with a diameter of 1 inch and a height of 6 inches. What is the volume of the unused space in the box, to the nearest tenth of an inch?

A 24.09 cu in.

B 22.01 cu in.

C 14.7 cu in.

D 1.66 cu in.

6.

What is the surface area of the given solid?

F 250π

G 300π

H 400π

J 500π

7. A cone has a radius of 7 centimeters and volume of 245π cubic centimeters.

What is the height of the cone?

A 15 cm

B 11.6 cm

C 32.6 cm

D 35 cm

8. Find the volume of the solid below.

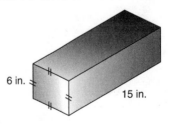

F 180 cu in.

G 360 cu in.

H 540 cu in.

J 1,080 cu in.

9. A triangular prism has a base area of $16\sqrt{3}$ square meters.

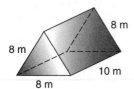

Find the surface area of this solid.

A $(240 + 32\sqrt{3})$ m²
B $(240 + 16\sqrt{3})$ m²
C $(192 + 32\sqrt{3})$ m²
D $(192 + 16\sqrt{3})$ m²

10. The solid below is a combination of a prism and a regular pyramid.

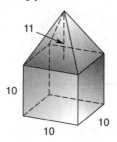

The volume of the solid is __?__.

F 700 cubic units
G 1,033.33 cubic units
H 1,366.67 cubic units
J 2,100 cubic units

PRACTICE 22   Similar Geometric Objects

Objective:	SOL G.14

☐ **The student will**
  a) **Use proportional reasoning to solve practical problems, given similar geometric objects; and**
  b) **Determine how changes in one dimension of an object affect area and/or volume of the object.**

Similar Objects   Similar objects are objects having the same shape but not necessarily the same size. These objects can be two-dimensional (polygons) or three-dimensional (solids).

Similar Pentagons

Similar Cylinders

REMEMBER

The ratio of any two corresponding lengths is also called the scale factor.

Two polygons are similar when corresponding angles are congruent and corresponding sides are proportional (the ratios of corresponding sides are equal). Two solids are similar when the bases are the same shape and corresponding lengths are proportional (the ratios of corresponding lengths are equal). When two figures are similar, the common ratio is called the **scale factor**.

Model Problem 1   Determine if each pair of objects is similar.

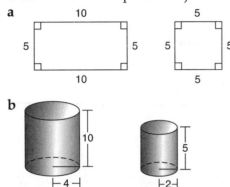

Solution a These two objects are polygons. Check if corresponding angles are congruent and the lengths of corresponding sides are proportional.

- Corresponding angles are congruent since they each measure 90°.
- However, corresponding sides are not proportional since the ratios of corresponding sides are not all equal.

$$\frac{\text{right side of the rectangle}}{\text{right side of the square}} = \frac{5}{5} = \frac{1}{1}$$

$$\frac{\text{bottom of the rectangle}}{\text{bottom of the square}} = \frac{10}{5} = \frac{2}{1}$$

Therefore, since the scale factors are not the same, the figures are not similar.

b These two objects are solids. Check if the bases have the same shape and if corresponding lengths are proportional.

- Both solids have circular bases.
- Corresponding lengths are proportional since the ratios of corresponding lengths are the same.

$$\frac{\text{radius of the larger cylinder}}{\text{radius of the smaller cylinder}} = \frac{4}{2} = \frac{2}{1}$$

$$\frac{\text{height of the larger cylinder}}{\text{height of the smaller cylinder}} = \frac{10}{5} = \frac{2}{1}$$

The scale factors are the same. Therefore, the solids are similar.

Note: Any two circles are similar. Also, any two spheres are similar.

Applications of Similarity Using the fact that two objects are similar, we can use the scale factor to find a missing measurement.

Model Problem 2 The figures below are similar.

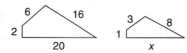

    a Find the scale factor.
    b Find the value of *x*.

Solution   **a** Using two corresponding sides, we see that the scale factor is $\frac{2}{1}$.

    b Write a proportion involving the scale factor, the missing length (*x*), and its corresponding length.

$$\frac{2}{1} = \frac{20}{x}$$
$$2x = 20$$
$$x = 10$$

The theorem below states the relationship between the scale factor, perimeters, areas, and volumes of similar objects.

If the Scale Factor of Two Similar Objects Is *a* : *b*, Then
- The ratio of corresponding perimeters is *a* : *b*.
- The ratio of the base areas, lateral areas, and surface areas is $a^2 : b^2$.
- The ratio of the volumes is $a^3 : b^3$.

Note: Lateral area is the surface area of an object minus the area of the base(s).

Model Problem 3 The two cylinders are similar.

What is the ratio of the surface areas of the cylinders?

Solution The scale factor = 4 : 2 or 2 : 1. Therefore, the ratio of the surface areas = $2^2 : 1^2$ or 4 : 1.

Model Problem 4 Two similar objects have a scale factor of 2 : 3. If the smaller object has a surface area of 36 square centimeters, what is the surface area of the larger object?

Solution Let x = the area of the larger object.
By the theorem, the ratio of the surface areas = $2^2 : 3^2$ or 4 : 9.
Write a proportion involving this ratio, the missing area (x), and the area of the smaller object.

$$\frac{4}{9} = \frac{36}{x}$$
$$4x = 36 \cdot 9$$
$$4x = 324$$
$$x = 81$$

Therefore, the area of the larger figure is 81 square centimeters.

How Changes in One Dimension Affect Area and Volume

The last concept discussed in this practice is determining how changes in one dimension affect the surface area and/or volume of an object.

Model Problem 5 A cone has a radius of 3 inches and a height of 10 inches. If the radius is doubled and the height remains the same, how does the volume of the new cone compare to the volume of the original cone?

Solution

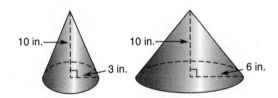

Volume of the original cone:

$r = 3$ in.

$h = 10$ in.

$V = \frac{1}{3}r^2h = \frac{1}{3}(3)^2(10) = \frac{1}{3}(9)(10) = \frac{1}{3}(90) = 30$ cu in.

Volume of the new cone:
If the radius is doubled, then $r = 6$ inches.
The height stays the same, so $h = 10$ inches.

$V = \frac{1}{3}(6)^2(10) = \frac{1}{3}(36)(10) = \frac{1}{3}(360) = 120$ cu in.

Therefore, if the radius of the cone is doubled, the volume of the new cone is $\frac{120}{30} = 4$ times the original volume.

1. Two cones have radii of 6 and 15 and heights of 10 and 25, respectively. Determine if the cones are similar.

2. Two similar rectangular prisms have lateral areas of 432 and 192 square inches. Find the ratio of the heights.

3. Two similar cylinders have heights of 10 and 25. If the volume of the smaller cylinder is 32π, what is the volume of the larger cylinder?

4. Are these solids similar?

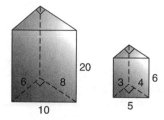

5. What will happen to the volume of the prism when you double its height?

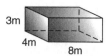

ASSESSMENT

1. The ratio of two similar polygons is 6 : 4. If the perimeter of the larger polygon is 27 feet, what is the perimeter of the smaller polygon?

    A 40.5 feet

    B 32 feet

    C 18 feet

    D 13.5 feet

2. A sphere has a radius of 3. If the radius is doubled, the volume of the new sphere is —

    F 2 times greater than the original sphere.

    G 4 times greater than the original sphere.

    H 6 times greater than the original sphere.

    J 8 times greater than the original sphere.

3. **Given:** Cylinder A similar to cylinder B with the surface area of cylinder A equal to 144π.

    The surface area of cylinder B is _?_ .

    A 256π

    B 192π

    C 152π

    D 144π

4. Two spheres have diameters of 20 and 36. What is the ratio of the surface areas?

    F 5 : 9

    G 10 : 18

    H 25 : 81

    J 125 : 729

5. If the height of a rectangular prism is increased from 2 feet to 8 feet, what effect does this have on the lateral area of the prism?

    A The lateral area is 2 times greater.

    B The lateral area is 4 times greater.

    C The lateral area is 6 times greater.

    D The lateral area is 8 times greater.

6. Two spheres have radii of 5 and 4. Find the ratio of the volumes.

    F 5 : 4

    G 25 : 16

    H 100 : 81

    J 125 : 64

7. What is the ratio of the radii of two similar cones if the ratio of the lateral areas is 25 : 16?

    A 5 : 4

    B 10 : 8

    C 25 : 16

    D 125 : 64

8. Two similar cylinders have surface areas of 81π and 144π. What is the ratio of the heights of the cylinders?

    F 3 : 4

    G 9 : 16

    H 81 : 144

    J 243 : 1,024

9. What is the ratio of the heights of two similar solids if the ratio of the volumes is 125 : 343?

    A 125 : 343

    B 50 : 98

    C 25 : 49

    D 5 : 7

10. The pyramid below is a square pyramid.

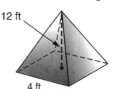

    If the base edges of the pyramid are tripled, what effect does this have on the volume of the pyramid?

    F The volume is 9 times greater.

    G The volume is 6 times greater.

    H The volume is 4 times greater.

    J The volume is 3 times greater.

PRACTICE 23   Cumulative Practice on SOLs G.12, 13, and 14

1. What is the surface area of a cube with one edge that is 9 centimeters long?

    A 324 cm^2

    B 486 cm^2

    C 648 cm^2

    D 729 cm^2

2. The distance between two cities is 630 miles. If 1 centimeter is equal to 75 miles, how far apart are the two cities on the map?

    F 9.4 cm

    G 9.0 cm

    H 8.4 cm

    J 8.0 cm

3. A sphere has a radius of 8. If the radius is doubled, what effect does this have on the surface area of the sphere?

    A The surface area is 2 times greater.

    B The surface area is 4 times greater.

    C The surface area is 6 times greater.

    D The surface area is 8 times greater.

4. One edge of a cube is 9 meters long. The volume is __?__.

   F 324 m³

   G 486 m³

   H 640 m³

   J 729 m³

5. Two similar cylinders have heights of 8 and 16. What is the ratio of the surface areas?

   A 3 : 2

   B 1 : 8

   C 1 : 4

   D 1 : 2

6.

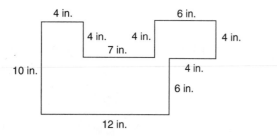

This is a floor plan of a house. If 7 feet = 1 inch, what is the actual perimeter of the house?

   F 61 inches

   G 61 feet

   H $8\frac{5}{7}$ feet

   J 427 feet

7. What is the scale factor of two similar solids if the ratio of the surface areas is 225 : 256?

   A 5 : 4

   B 25 : 16

   C 15 : 16

   D 225 : 256

8.

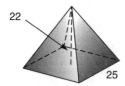

Find the volume of the square pyramid.

   F $183\frac{1}{3}$ cubic units

   G $4,033\frac{1}{3}$ cubic units

   H $4,233\frac{1}{3}$ cubic units

   J $4,583\frac{1}{3}$ cubic units

9. Which shows the top view of the figure below?

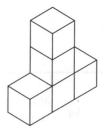

   A

   B

   C

   D

10. The regular prism below has a height of 10 and a base edge of 8.

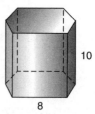

What is the lateral area of the prism?

   F 360 square units

   G 480 square units

   H 640 square units

   J 800 square units

11. The scale factor of two similar polygons is 2 : 3. If the surface area of the smaller polygon is 36 square meters, what is the surface area of the larger polygon?

A 16 m²

B 24 m²

C 54 m²

D 81 m²

12. This is one view of a 3-dimensional object.

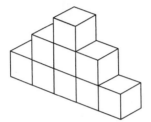

Which is a different view of the same object?

F

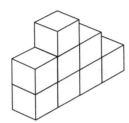

G

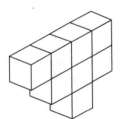

H

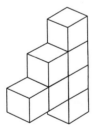

J

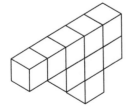

13. The ratio of the volumes of two similar pyramids is 125 : 343. The scale factor of the two pyramids is ? .

A 5 : 7

B 7 : 5

C 25 : 49

D 125 : 343

14. The front and side views of a solid figure are given below.

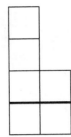

Front view

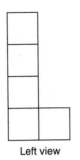 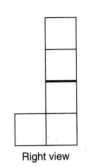

Left view   Right view

Which shows the back view?

F

G

H

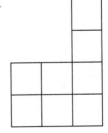

J

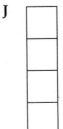

15. The dimensions of a box are 12 inches by 7.5 inches by 4.5 inches.

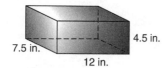

How many square inches of wrapping paper will you need to cover the sides and bottom of the box?

A 355.3 sq in.

B 367.75 sq in.

C 265.5 sq in.

D 1,178.75 sq in.

16. The following pattern is that of a __?__ .

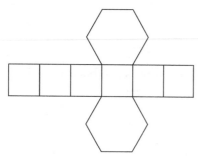

F Pentagonal prism

G Hexagonal prism

H Heptagonal prism

J Octagonal prism

17.

What is the volume of the sphere?

A 36π

B 20.25π

C 12π

D 6.75π

18. Find the ratio of the lateral areas of the two similar solids.

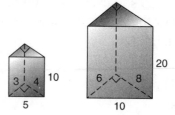

F 1 : 2

G 1 : 4

H 1 : 8

J 1 : 16

19. A cone has a volume of 96π.

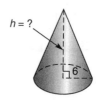

If the radius of the cone is 6, what is the height of the cone?

A 24

B 16

C 12

D 8

20. The Washington Monument is 169.29 meters tall. If a scale model is built using a scale where 5 meters = 1 inch, what is the height of the scale model?

F 30.66 in.

G 30.78 in.

H 33.75 in.

J 33.86 in.

21. Pyramids *A* and *B* are similar.

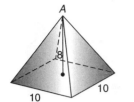

If the volume of pyramid *A* is $\frac{800}{3}$ cubic units, what is the volume of pyramid *B*?

A $\frac{1,600}{3}$ cubic units

B $\frac{400}{3}$ cubic units

C $\frac{200}{3}$ cubic units

D $\frac{100}{3}$ cubic units

22.

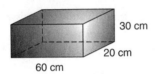

If the length of the rectangle base is decreased from 60 centimeters to 20 centimeters, what effect does this have on the volume of the rectangular prism?

F The volume is cut in half.

G The volume is one-third smaller.

H The volume is one-fourth smaller.

J The volume is one-fifth smaller.

23. The solid below consists of a cylinder and a cone.

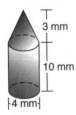

What is the volume of the solid?

A 138.16 mm³

B 163.28 mm³

C 175.84 mm³

D 514.96 mm³

24. Which shows the front view of this solid?

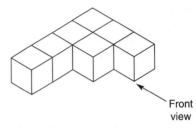

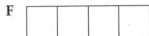

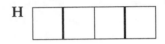

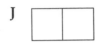

25.

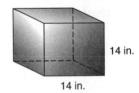

If each edge of the cube is decreased by one-half, what effect does this have on the surface area of the cube?

A The surface area is two times smaller.

B The surface area is three times smaller.

C The surface area is four times smaller.

D The surface area is six times smaller.

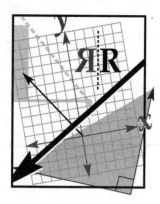

UNIT 5
Coordinate Relations and Transformations

PRACTICE 24 Distance, Slopes, and Midpoints

Objective:	SOL G.2a

☐ The student will use pictorial representations, including computer software, constructions, and coordinate methods, to solve problems involving symmetry and transformation. This will include investigating and using formulas for finding distance, midpoint, and slope.

The Distance Formula The distance between two points on a number line is equal to the absolute value of the difference between the coordinates of the two points.

Example

Find the distance between C and D.

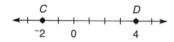

Solution

C is at $^-2$ and D is at 4. The distance between C and D is $|^-2 - 4| = |^-6| = 6$. Therefore, $CD = 6$.

The following formula gives us the distance between two points in a **plane** (a flat two-dimensional area).

> **Distance Formula**
>
> The distance between two points (x_1, y_1) and (x_2, y_2) is
> $$D = \sqrt{(x_2 - x_1)^2 + (y_2 - y_1)^2}$$

The Distance Formula is an application of the Pythagorean Theorem $a^2 + b^2 = c^2$. Find the distance between E and F by letting $EF = c$, $EG = a$, and $FG = b$.

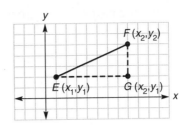

Substituting these values into the Pythagorean Theorem, we have:

$$(EF)^2 = (EG)^2 + (FG)^2$$
$$(EF)^2 = (x_2 - x_1)^2 + (y_2 - y_1)^2$$
$$EF = \sqrt{(x_2 - x_1)^2 + (y_2 - y_1)^2}$$

Therefore, the general formula for finding the distance between two points is
$$D = \sqrt{(x_2 - x_1)^2 + (y_2 - y_1)^2}$$

Model Problem 1   Point A is located at $(2, {}^-1)$ and point B is located at $(3, 3)$. Find the distance between A and B.

Solution   Let $A(2, {}^-1) = (x_1, y_1)$ and $B(3, 3) = (x_2, y_2)$.
Substitute these points into the formula $D = \sqrt{(x_2 - x_1)^2 + (y_2 - y_1)^2}$.
$$D = \sqrt{(3 - 2)^2 + (3 - ({}^-1))^2} = \sqrt{(1)^2 + (3 + 1)^2}$$
$$D = \sqrt{1 + 16} = \sqrt{17} \approx 4.12$$
Therefore, the distance between the two points is $\sqrt{17}$ units or approximately 4.12 units.

The Slope of a Line   In reviewing the concept of slope, the following topics will be discussed:

- The definition of slope.
- Finding the slope.
- The physical interpretation of slope.
- The slopes of parallel or perpendicular lines.

The **slope** of a line is a measure of the "steepness" of the line.

Slope Formula

The slope (m) of the line containing the points (x_1, y_1) and (x_2, y_2) is

$$m = \frac{y_2 - y_1}{x_2 - x_1} \text{ or } \frac{y_1 - y_2}{x_1 - x_2} \text{ or } \frac{\text{rise}}{\text{run}}$$

Model Problem 2   Find the slope of the line containing $(4, 5)$ and $({}^-7, 10)$.

Solution   Let $(x_1, y_1) = (4, 5)$ and $(x_2, y_2) = ({}^-7, 10)$.
$$m = \frac{y_2 - y_1}{x_2 - x_1} = \frac{10 - 5}{{}^-7 - 4} = \frac{5}{{}^-11}$$

Therefore, the slope is $\frac{{}^-5}{11}$.

Model Problem 3   What is the slope of this line?

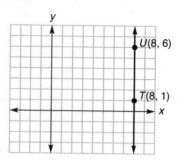

Solution   Let $T(8, 1) = (x_1, y_1)$ and $U(8, 6) = (x_2, y_2)$.

$$m = \frac{y_2 - y_1}{x_2 - x_1} = \frac{6 - 1}{8 - 8} = \frac{5}{0}$$

We say that the slope is undefined (not zero) because division by zero is undefined. When does the slope of a line equal zero?

The following table will help you understand slope.

GRAPH	INTERPRETATION	WHICH MEANS
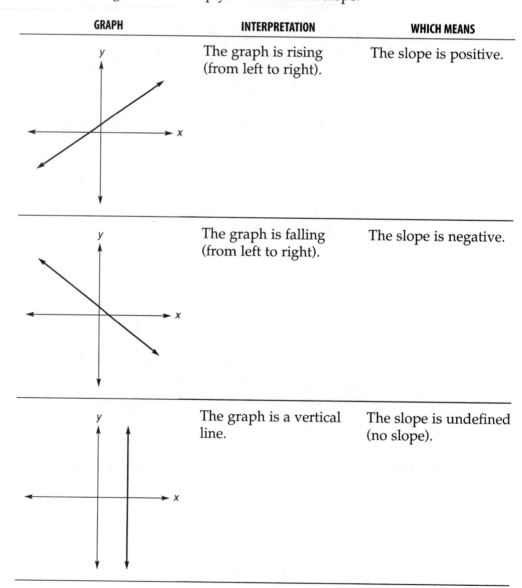	The graph is rising (from left to right).	The slope is positive.
	The graph is falling (from left to right).	The slope is negative.
	The graph is a vertical line.	The slope is undefined (no slope).

(continued)

GRAPH	INTERPRETATION	WHICH MEANS
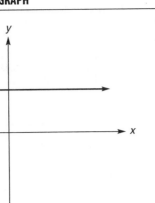	The graph is a horizontal line.	The slope is equal to zero.

Model Problem 4   **Given:** $A(2, 6)$, $B(5, 10)$, $C(3, 2)$, and $D(6, 6)$ with $\overleftrightarrow{AB}$ parallel to $\overleftrightarrow{CD}$.

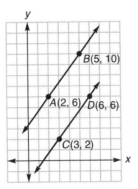

Find the slope of each line and make a conjecture about the slopes of parallel lines.

Solution

SLOPE OF $\overleftrightarrow{AB}$

Let $A(2, 6) = (x_1, y_1)$ and $B(5, 10) = (x_2, y_2)$.

slope of $\overleftrightarrow{AB} = \dfrac{y_2 - y_1}{x_2 - x_1}$

slope of $\overleftrightarrow{AB} = \dfrac{10 - 6}{5 - 2}$

slope of $\overleftrightarrow{AB} = \dfrac{4}{3}$

SLOPE OF $\overleftrightarrow{CD}$

Let $C(3, 2) = (x_1, y_1)$ and $D(6, 6) = (x_2, y_2)$.

slope of $\overleftrightarrow{CD} = \dfrac{y_2 - y_1}{x_2 - x_1}$

slope of $\overleftrightarrow{CD} = \dfrac{6 - 2}{6 - 3}$

slope of $\overleftrightarrow{CD} = \dfrac{4}{3}$

The slopes are equal.
Conjecture: *Parallel lines have equal slopes.*

Model Problem 5   Given: $W(4, 9)$, $U(6, 12)$, $S(3, 6)$, and $R(0, 8)$ with $\overleftrightarrow{WU}$ perpendicular to $\overleftrightarrow{SR}$.

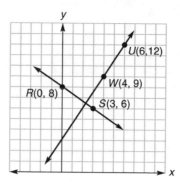

Find the slope of each line and make a conjecture about the slopes of perpendicular lines.

Solution

SLOPE OF $\overleftrightarrow{WU}$

Let $W(4, 9) = (x_1, y_1)$ and $U(6, 12) = (x_2, y_2)$.

$$\text{slope of } \overleftrightarrow{WU} = \frac{y_2 - y_1}{x_2 - x_1}$$

$$\text{slope of } \overleftrightarrow{WU} = \frac{12 - 9}{6 - 4}$$

$$\text{slope of } \overleftrightarrow{WU} = \frac{3}{2}$$

SLOPE OF $\overleftrightarrow{SR}$

Let $S(3, 6) = (x_1, y_1)$ and $R(0, 8) = (x_2, y_2)$.

$$\text{slope of } \overleftrightarrow{SR} = \frac{y_2 - y_1}{x_2 - x_1}$$

$$\text{slope of } \overleftrightarrow{SR} = \frac{8 - 6}{0 - 3}$$

$$\text{slope of } \overleftrightarrow{SR} = \frac{2}{-3}$$

The slopes are negative reciprocals of each other.
Conjecture: *Perpendicular lines have slopes that are negative reciprocals.*

In fact, the conjectures from the previous Model Problems are true.

Theorems Concerning Parallel and Perpendicular Lines

- Parallel lines have equal slopes. Conversely, if the slopes are equal, then the lines are parallel.

- Two perpendicular lines have slopes that are negative reciprocals. Conversely, if the slopes of two lines are negative reciprocals, then the two lines are perpendicular.

The Midpoint Formula   The **midpoint** of a line segment is the point that divides the segment into two equal parts. On a number line, the midpoint of the segment joining two points, x_1 and x_2, is equal to the average of the coordinates of the two points, $\frac{x_1 + x_2}{2}$.

Example

Find the coordinate of the midpoint.

Solution

The midpoint $= \dfrac{x_2 + x_2}{2} = \dfrac{1 + 7}{2} = \dfrac{8}{2} = 4$.

Therefore, the coordinate of the midpoint is 4.

In a plane, the midpoint of the segment joining two points is found by averaging both the x and y coordinates of the two points.

Midpoint Formula

The coordinates of the midpoint (M) of the segment joining (x_1, y_1) and (x_2, y_2) are

$$M = \left(\underbrace{\frac{x_1 + x_2}{2}}_{\substack{\text{average of the} \\ x \text{ coordinates}}} , \underbrace{\frac{y_1 + y_2}{2}}_{\substack{\text{average of the} \\ y \text{ coordinates}}} \right)$$

Model Problem 6   Find the coordinates of the midpoint of the line segment joining $(4, 6)$ and $(10, {}^-4)$.

Solution   Let $(x_1, y_1) = (4, 6)$ and $(x_2, y_2) = (10, {}^-4)$.

$$M = \left(\frac{x_1 + x_2}{2}, \frac{y_1 + y_2}{2} \right) = \left(\frac{4 + 10}{2}, \frac{6 + {}^-4}{2} \right) = \left(\frac{14}{2}, \frac{2}{2} \right) = (7, 1)$$

Therefore, the coordinates of the midpoint are $(7, 1)$.

 TRY THESE

1. Find the slope of the line that contains $({}^-5, 2)$ and $(4, 6)$.

2. Find the distance between $(10, 3)$ and $(10, 5)$.

3. Find the coordinates of the midpoint of the segment joining $A(4, 7)$ and $E({}^-2, 5)$.

4. **Given:** $\overline{GI}$ with $G(4, 5)$ and $I(9, 10)$; $\overline{JK}$ with $J(8, 14)$ and $K(3, 9)$.
   Without drawing the two lines, determine if $\overline{GI}$ is parallel to $\overline{JK}$ or if $\overline{GI}$ is perpendicular to $\overline{JK}$.

5. Find the slope of the segment that joins $J(6, {}^-7)$ and $B({}^-3, {}^-7)$.

6. **Given:** $\overline{AB}$ with $A(2, {}^-1)$ and $B(1, 7)$; $\overline{CD}$ with $C({}^-2, 2)$ and $D(5, 4)$.
   Determine if $\overline{AB}$ is perpendicular to $\overline{CD}$.

7. Find the distance between $(3, 5)$ and $(15, 11)$.

8. **Given:** Trapezoid $ABCD$ with median $\overline{EF}$.

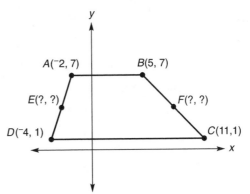

Find the coordinates of E and F.

Hint: The median is the line segment that joins the midpoints of the legs. Hence, E is the midpoint of $\overline{AD}$ and F is the midpoint of $\overline{BC}$.

1. What is the slope of the line that passes through ($^-$4, 6) and (3, 1)?

    A $\frac{7}{5}$

    B $\frac{5}{7}$

    C $\frac{^-5}{7}$

    D $\frac{^-7}{5}$

2. Which represents the distance between A(4, 7) and B($^-$3, $^-$5), to the nearest hundredth?

    F 2.24

    G 7.35

    H 12.04

    J 13.89

3. What are the coordinates of the midpoint of $\overline{CD}$ if C = (5, 8) and D = ($^-$10, $^-$15)?

    A $\left(2\frac{1}{2}, 3\frac{1}{2}\right)$

    B $\left(7\frac{1}{2}, 11\frac{1}{2}\right)$

    C $\left(11\frac{1}{2}, 7\frac{1}{2}\right)$

    D $\left(^-2\frac{1}{2}, ^-3\frac{1}{2}\right)$

4. **Given:** W(5, 3), X(3, $^-$1), Y(4, 10), and Z(6, 9). The slopes of $\overline{WX}$ and $\overline{YZ}$ are ? .

    F equal

    G reciprocals

    H negative reciprocals

    J undefined

5. What is the slope of the line containing (3, 7) and (8, 7)?

    A 0

    B $\frac{14}{11}$

    C $\frac{14}{5}$

    D Undefined

6. The distance between D(7, 5) and C(3, 2) is ? .

    F 1

    G 5

    H 7

    J 25

7. The coordinates of the midpoint of the segment joining X(10, $^-$3) and Y(4, $^-$9) are ? .

    A (3, 3)

    B (3, $^-$3)

    C (7, $^-$6)

    D ($^-$7, $^-$6)

8. What is the slope of the line that passes through the points $\left(1, ^-2\frac{1}{2}\right)$ and $\left(9, \frac{1}{2}\right)$?

    F $\frac{1}{4}$

    G $\frac{3}{8}$

    H $\frac{3}{10}$

    J 4

9. What is the slope of a line parallel to $\overline{WZ}$ if W = ($^-$4, $^-$3) and Z = (7, $^-$1)?

    A $\frac{11}{2}$

    B $\frac{2}{11}$

    C $\frac{^-2}{11}$

    D $\frac{^-11}{2}$

10. Given T = (2, 0) and U = ($^-$2, 0), what are the coordinates of the midpoint of the segment joining these two points?

    F (0, 0)

    G (0, $^-$2)

    H (1, 1)

    J (2, 0)

PRACTICE 25 Symmetry and Transformations

Objective:	SOL G.2b

☐ The student will use pictorial representations including computer software, constructions, and coordinate methods, to solve problems involving symmetry and transformation. This will include investigating the symmetry of a figure and determining whether a figure is symmetric with respect to a line or a point.

A figure has **symmetry** if it remains unchanged by an operation such as a reflection or a rotation. For example, the letter Z is symmetric with respect to its center since it looks the same when rotated 180° about its center.

Reflection Symmetry

An object has **reflection** or **line symmetry** if it can be divided into two congruent parts (with each part the mirror image of the other). For example, the letter B has reflection symmetry about a vertical line.

B
line of
symmetry

To test an object for reflection symmetry, trace the object on a piece of patty paper and see if it can be folded into two congruent parts. The line on the fold is called the **line of symmetry**. Another way to test for reflection symmetry is to use a mirror or a geo-reflector, which is placed on the figure so that one-half of the figure and its reflection appear to complete the object. For example, a rectangle has line symmetry.

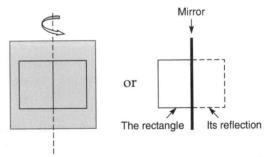

Some figures have no line symmetry. Some have one line of symmetry while others may have two or more lines of symmetry. The circle is an example of a figure that has infinitely many lines of symmetry, since there are an infinite number of diameters that can be drawn on the circle. (Remember, a diameter cuts a circle into two equal halves.)

Model Problem 1   Identify the lines of symmetry in the figures below.

a

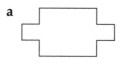

b

c

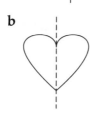

Solution   **a**

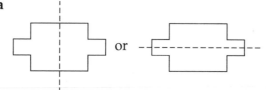   This polygon has a vertical and a horizontal line of symmetry.

b

   The heart has a vertical line of symmetry.

c No lines of symmetry.

Point and Rotational Symmetry   A figure has **rotational symmetry** if the traced figure can be rotated (less than 360°) around some fixed point so that it looks like the original figure. For example, a daisy has rotational symmetry with respect to its center.

Rotate   Result of rotation

REMEMBER

A figure has **point symmetry** if it has 180° rotational symmetry about its center.

To test a figure for rotational symmetry (about a specific point), trace the figure on a piece of patty paper. Rotate the patty paper up to, but not including 360° about that point. If, while rotating the patty paper, the traced figure looks like the original figure (at least once), then the figure has rotational symmetry. For example, an equilateral triangle has 120° rotational symmetry about its center.

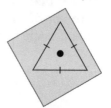

Rotate 120°   Result of rotation

Model Problem 2   Identify the figure with rotational symmetry.

a

Isosceles trapezoid

b

Solution   **a** This polygon does not have rotational symmetry. No matter how much we rotate this polygon (up to, but not including 360°) the rotated image never looks like the original figure.

   b This figure has rotational symmetry since it is unchanged by a 90° rotation.

Rotate 90°   Result of
                    90° rotation

Please note that this figure also has point symmetry since it is unchanged by a 180° rotation (around its center).

 TRY THESE

1. How many lines of symmetry does this figure have?

2. Does the figure below have rotational symmetry?

3. This kite has how many lines of symmetry?

4. How many lines of symmetry does this figure have? Does it also have point symmetry?

5. The letter J has how many lines of symmetry?

6. Identify the phrase with both line and point symmetry.
   a **XOOXOOX**
   b **HDEOEDH**

7. Does this polygon have point symmetry?

 ＡＳＳＥＳＳＭＥＮＴ

1. How many lines of symmetry does the letter D have?

   A One
   B Two
   C Three
   D Four

2. What is true about this figure?

   F The figure has a horizontal line of symmetry only.
   G The figure has a vertical line of symmetry only.
   H The figure has both line and point symmetry.
   J The figure has point symmetry but no line symmetry.

3. How many lines of symmetry does a square have?
   A One
   B Two
   C Three
   D Four

4. Identify all of the types of symmetry that can be found in this polygon.

F Vertical symmetry and point symmetry
G Vertical symmetry only
H Horizontal symmetry only
J Both vertical and horizontal symmetry

5. How many lines of symmetry does an ellipse have?

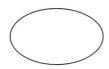

A Two
B Three
C Four
D Infinite

6. Which of the following have point symmetry?

I

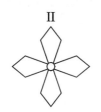

II

III

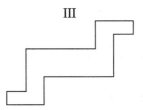

F Figures I and II
G Figures I and III
H Figures II and III
J Figures I, II, and III

7. This star has how many lines of symmetry?

A One
B Three
C Four
D Five

8.

DOB

The phrase "DOB" has —
F a horizontal line of symmetry only.
G both a horizontal line of symmetry and point symmetry.
H point symmetry only.
J no symmetry.

9. The figure below has ? .

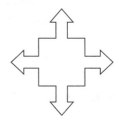

A line symmetry only
B point symmetry only
C both line and point symmetry
D no symmetry

10. The figure below has ? .

F line symmetry
G point symmetry
H both line and point symmetry
J no symmetry

PRACTICE 26 Applications Involving Transformations

Objective:	SOL G.2c

❑ The student will use pictorial representations, including computer software, constructions, and coordinate methods to solve problems involving symmetry and transformation. This will include determining whether a figure has been translated, reflected, or rotated.

Transformations

A figure in a plane can be reflected, rotated, or translated to produce a new figure congruent to the original figure. The new figure is called the **image** and the original figure is called the **preimage**.

Example

The preimage is $\triangle ABC$, and the image is $\triangle A'B'C'$, the original triangle after a translation.

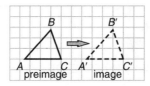

A **transformation** is an operation mapping a preimage onto an image. A **congruence transformation** (or an **isometry**) is a transformation that maps a preimage onto a *congruent* image. Reflections, rotations, translations, and any combination of these are the only congruence transformations.

Reflections

A **reflection** is a transformation in which an object is flipped over a line called the **line of reflection**. In a reflection, the image and the preimage have opposite orientations and are congruent.

Model Problem 1

Which of the following show a reflection?

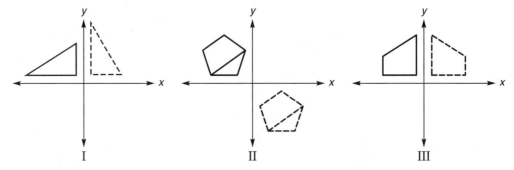

I	II	III

Solution

I   Figure I does not show a reflection because the two triangles do not have opposite orientations.

II   Figure II does not show a reflection because the two pentagons do not have opposite orientations.

III   Figure III shows a single reflection since the two quadrilaterals have opposite orientations and are congruent.

Translations In a **translation** or a **slide**, an object is shifted in a specified direction and distance (with no change in size). Unlike a reflection, the image and the preimage have the same orientation.

Example

Model Problem 2 Translate $\triangle ABC$ with $A(^-3, 1)$, $B(^-5, 5)$, and $C(3, 7)$ to the right by 8 units. What are the coordinates of the image $\triangle A'B'C'$?

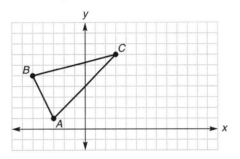

Solution

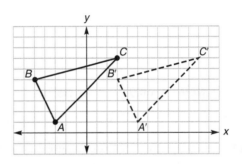

The coordinates are $A'(5, 1)$, $B'(3, 5)$, and $C'(11, 7)$.

> **Note:** Any translation can be accomplished by following one reflection by another with respect to two parallel lines. For example, in the figure below, the arrow is first reflected over line ℓ, then reflected over line m. The resulting image is a translation of the original arrow.
>
>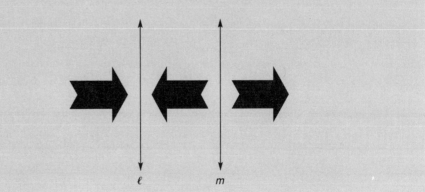

Reflections in the Coordinate Plane

For a reflection in a coordinate plane, the following rules can be used:

TYPE OF REFLECTION	POINT	BECOMES
Reflection over the x-axis	(a, b)	$(a, {}^{-}b)$
Reflection over the y-axis	(a, b)	$({}^{-}a, b)$
Reflection over the $y = x$ line	(a, b)	(b, a)
Reflection over the $y = {}^{-}x$ line	(a, b)	$({}^{-}b, {}^{-}a)$
Point reflection at the origin $(0, 0)$	(a, b)	$({}^{-}a, {}^{-}b)$

Rotations

The last type of transformation that will be discussed is called a **rotation**. When a rotation occurs, the object is revolved around a fixed point called the **center of rotation**. The **angle of rotation** is the angle about which the object is rotated.

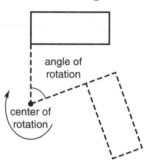

Note: A rotation can be clockwise or counterclockwise.

Model Problem 3 Which of the following show a rotation around the point P?

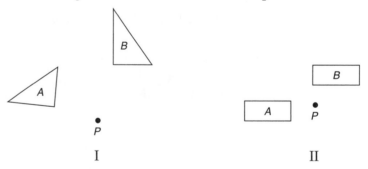

Solution I Step 1. Trace triangle *A* and point *P* onto a piece of patty paper.

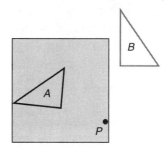

Step 2. Rotate the patty paper clockwise or counterclockwise around the point *P*. Try to match triangle *B* with the traced triangle. If a match can be made, then you have a rotation.

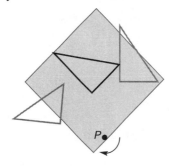

Step 3. Triangle *A* matches triangle *B*.

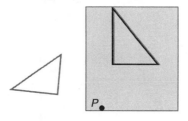

Therefore, figure I shows a rotation about *P*.

II Follow the steps for figure I.

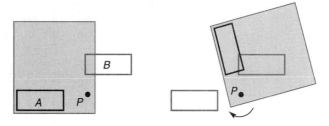

No matter how much we rotate rectangle *A* about *P*, the rotated figure never matches rectangle *B*. Therefore, figure II does not show a rotation.

Any rotation can be accomplished by following one reflection by another with respect to two intersecting lines. The point of intersection corresponds to the center of rotation. The measure of the angle of rotation equals twice the measure of the angle formed by the two intersecting lines.

Example

Rotate △*DEF* clockwise by reflecting over line *t* and then line ℓ.

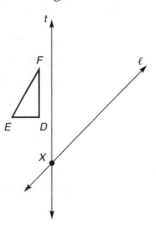

Solution

Step 1.   Trace △*DEF* and lines *t* and ℓ onto a piece of patty paper.
Step 2.   Fold the patty paper along line *t*, and trace △*DEF* to form △*D′E′F′*.

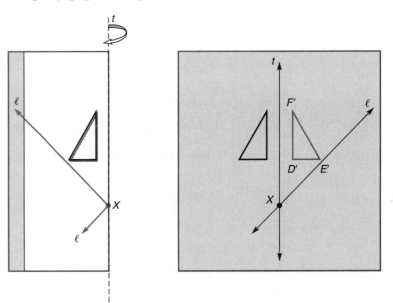

△*D′E′F′* is the reflection of △*DEF* over line *t*.

Step 3. Fold the patty paper along line ℓ, and trace $\triangle D'E'F'$ to form $\triangle D''E''F''$.

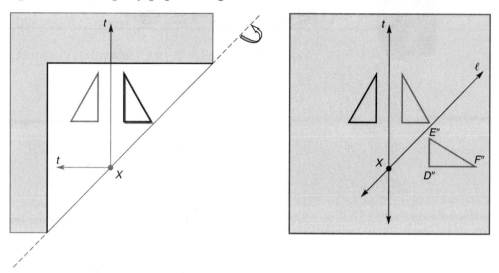

$\triangle D''E''F''$ is the reflection of $\triangle D'E'F'$ over line ℓ.

The resulting triangle is a rotation of $\triangle DEF$ around the point X.

Rotations in the Coordinate Plane   For a rotation about the origin in a coordinate plane, the following rules can be used:

TURN TYPE (COUNTERCLOCKWISE)	ROTATION	POINT	BECOMES
Quarter-turn	90°	(a, b)	$(^-b, a)$
Half-turn	180°	(a, b)	$(^-a, ^-b)$
Three-quarter-turn	270°	(a, b)	$(b, ^-a)$

Model Problem 4   Rotate $ABCD$ with $A(4, 0)$, $B(^-5, 2)$, $C(3, 1)$, $D(8, ^-2)$ counterclockwise 180° about the origin.

Solution   A 180° counterclockwise rotation about the origin will change the point (a, b) to $(^-a, ^-b)$.

$$A(4, 0) \rightarrow A'(^-4, 0)$$
$$B(^-5, 2) \rightarrow B'(5, ^-2)$$
$$C(3, 1) \rightarrow C'(^-3, ^-1)$$
$$D(8, ^-2) \rightarrow D'(^-8, 2)$$

1. Which rectangle (*A*, *B*, or *C*) is a rotation of rectangle I around the point *P*?

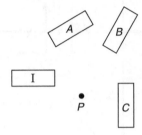

2. Which triangle (*A*, *B*, or *C*) is a translation of triangle II?

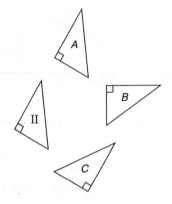

3. Tell whether the figure shows a translation.

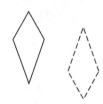

4. Reflect the trapezoid over the *x*-axis, and then over the *y*-axis.

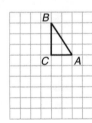

5. Translate △*ABC* two units to the left and five units down.

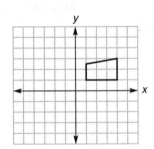

6. Rotate the rhombus 90° clockwise around the point L.

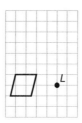

7. Reflect the half-circle over the line t.

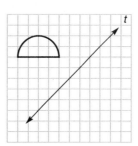

ASSESSMENT

1. Reflect $\triangle ABC$ with $A(^-3, 1)$, $B(1, 5)$, and $C(2, 1)$ over the x-axis. What are the coordinates of the image $\triangle A'B'C'$?

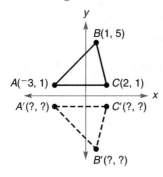

A $A'(^-3, ^-1)$, $B'(^-1, ^-5)$, $C'(^-2, ^-1)$

B $A'(^-3, ^-1)$, $B'(1, ^-5)$, $C'(^-2, ^-1)$

C $A'(^-3, ^-1)$, $B'(1, ^-5)$, $C'(2, ^-1)$

D $A'(^-3, 1)$, $B'(^-1, 5)$, $C'(2, 1)$

2.

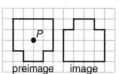

The image of the octagon can be obtained by a _?_.

F a reflection followed by a translation

G a rotation around the point P

H a single reflection

J a single translation

3. Which of the trapezoids can be obtained by a single reflection of trapezoid I?

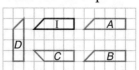

A Trapezoid A

B Trapezoid B

C Trapezoid C

D Trapezoid D

4. Which shows a 90° clockwise rotation of the letter N around the origin?

F
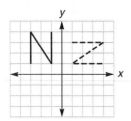

G
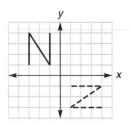

H
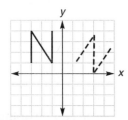

J
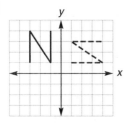

5. Under the translation Z: $(x, y) \Rightarrow (x + 3, y - 1)$, which means to translate the pre-image 3 units to the right and 1 unit down, what is the image of the point $(^-7, 2)$?

A $(^-4, ^-3)$

B $(^-4, 1)$

C $(4, 1)$

D $(4, 3)$

6. Suppose that a segment with endpoints $A(1, 2)$ and $B(^-2, 5)$ is rotated counterclockwise around the origin by 180°.

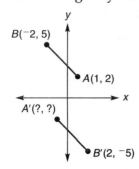

If the image of B is $(2, ^-5)$, what is the image of A?

F $(1, 2)$

G $(^-1, ^-2)$

H $(^-2, ^-1)$

J $(^-2, ^-2)$

7. The reflection over __?__ sends the point $(^-10, 2)$ to $(10, 2)$. Which replaces the "?" to make the statement true?

A the x-axis

B the y-axis

C the line $y = x$

D the line $y = ^-x$

8. What is the image of W after being reflected over the line t?

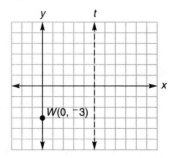

F $(5, ^-3)$

G $(10, ^-3)$

H $(10, 0)$

J $(10, 5)$

9. What is the image of $(^-4, 3)$ under a 90° counterclockwise rotation around the origin?

A $(^-4, ^-3)$

B $(^-4, ^-2)$

C $(^-3, ^-4)$

D $(4, ^-2)$

10.

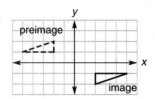

The figure shows —

F a translation.

G a reflection over the line $y = x$.

H a reflection over the x-axis.

J a 180° rotation around the origin.

1. The letter A has how many lines of symmetry?

A

A One
B Two
C Three
D Four

2. What are the coordinates of the midpoint of $\overline{CD}$ if $C = (2, 10)$ and $D = (^-7, 5)$?

F $(^-2.5, 7.5)$
G $(^-2.5, ^-7.5)$
H $(2.5, ^-7.5)$
J $(2.5, 2.5)$

3. The figure below shows an example of a ?.

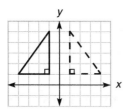

A a reflection and a rotation
B reflection
C rotation
D translation

4. What is the slope of the line that passes through the points $(^-6, 4)$ and $(^-5, 3)$?

F $^-1$
G $\dfrac{^-1}{11}$
H $\dfrac{1}{11}$
J 1

5. What is the distance between $A(^-4, 7)$ and $B(^-2, ^-9)$, to the nearest hundredth?

A 2.83
B 7.21
C 16.12
D 17.09

6.

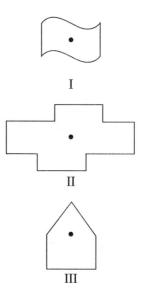

I

II

III

Which figures have point symmetry?

F I and II
G I and III
H II and III
J II only

7.

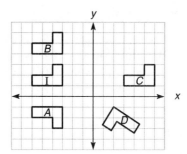

Which is a reflection of polygon I?

A Polygon A
B Polygon B
C Polygon C
D Polygon D

8. What is the slope of the line passing through $(7, 3)$ and $(7, 8)$?

F 0
G $\dfrac{14}{11}$
H $\dfrac{14}{5}$
J Undefined

9. Name all the types of symmetry that can be found in the figure below.

    A Horizontal symmetry

    B Vertical and horizontal symmetry

    C Vertical and point symmetry

    D Vertical symmetry

10. The distance between $D(12, 8)$ and $C(7, {}^-4)$ is ___?___.

    F 5

    G 6.5

    H 7

    J 13

11.

The polygon has —

    A a vertical line of symmetry only.

    B a horizontal line of symmetry only.

    C point and line symmetry.

    D point symmetry only.

12. Under the translation $A(x, y) \Rightarrow (x - 2, y + 2)$, which means to translate the pre-image two units to the left and two units up, what is the image of the point $({}^-5, 3)$?

    F $({}^-7, 5)$

    G $({}^-5, 3)$

    H $(3, 5)$

    J $(5, 3)$

13. The distance between $A(0, 8)$ and $B({}^-8, 10)$ is ___?___.

    A 8

    B 8.2

    C 11.3

    D 19.7

14. This figure shows a ___?___.

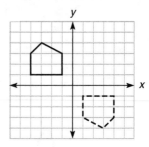

    F 90° rotation

    G 180° rotation

    H reflection

    J translation

15. Given points $T(4, 0)$ and $U({}^-8, 0)$, what are the coordinates of the midpoint of $\overline{TU}$?

    A $({}^-2, 0)$

    B $(0, {}^-2)$

    C $(0, 0)$

    D $(6, 0)$

16. What is the image of the point $(5, 8)$ under a reflection over the x-axis?

    F $({}^-5, {}^-8)$

    G $({}^-5, 8)$

    H $(5, {}^-8)$

    J $(8, 5)$

17. How many lines of symmetry does a regular pentagon have?

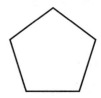

    A One

    B Two

    C Four

    D Five

18. Find the image of the point $A(^-2, 4)$ under a half-turn around the point $(1, 1)$.

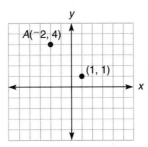

F $(^-2, ^-4)$

G $(^-2, 4)$

H $(2, ^-4)$

J $(4, ^-2)$

19. What is the slope of a line perpendicular to $\overline{WZ}$ if $W = (^-4, ^-3)$ and $Z = (7, ^-1)$?

A $\dfrac{11}{2}$

B $\dfrac{2}{11}$

C $\dfrac{^-2}{11}$

D $\dfrac{^-11}{2}$

20. A reflection maps $B(^-5, 2)$ to $B'(^-5, ^-2)$. Find the line of reflection.

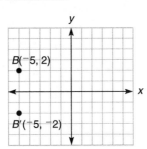

F The line $y = x$

G The y-axis

H The x-axis

J The line $y = ^-x$

21.

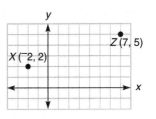

What is the distance between X and Z, to the nearest tenth?

A 11.4

B 9.5

C 8.6

D 5.8

22. What is the image of $(3, 6)$ under a 270° counterclockwise rotation around the origin?

F $(6, ^-3)$

G $(3, ^-6)$

H $(^-3, ^-6)$

J $(^-6, ^-6)$

23. The figure below has ___?___ .

A point symmetry only

B line symmetry only

C point and line symmetry

D no symmetry

24. Which of the following show a translation?

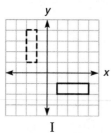

I

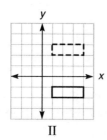

II

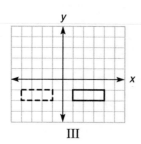

III

F I and II

G II and III

H II only

J III only

25. Given $X(8, {}^-2)$ and $Y(4, {}^-8)$, what are the coordinates of the midpoint of $\overline{XY}$?

A (6, 3)

B (6, ${}^-5$)

C (2, 3)

D (${}^-5$, 6)

Answer Sheet Sample Test A

Use a No. 2 pencil. Fill in the circle completely. If you erase, erase completely. Incomplete erasures may be read as answers.

1. Ⓐ Ⓑ Ⓒ Ⓓ   26. Ⓕ Ⓖ Ⓗ Ⓙ

2. Ⓕ Ⓖ Ⓗ Ⓙ   27. Ⓐ Ⓑ Ⓒ Ⓓ

3. Ⓐ Ⓑ Ⓒ Ⓓ   28. Ⓕ Ⓖ Ⓗ Ⓙ

4. Ⓕ Ⓖ Ⓗ Ⓙ   29. Ⓐ Ⓑ Ⓒ Ⓓ

5. Ⓐ Ⓑ Ⓒ Ⓓ   30. Ⓕ Ⓖ Ⓗ Ⓙ

6. Ⓕ Ⓖ Ⓗ Ⓙ   31. Ⓐ Ⓑ Ⓒ Ⓓ

7. Ⓐ Ⓑ Ⓒ Ⓓ   32. Ⓕ Ⓖ Ⓗ Ⓙ

8. Ⓕ Ⓖ Ⓗ Ⓙ   33. Ⓐ Ⓑ Ⓒ Ⓓ

9. Ⓐ Ⓑ Ⓒ Ⓓ   34. Ⓕ Ⓖ Ⓗ Ⓙ

10. Ⓕ Ⓖ Ⓗ Ⓙ   35. Ⓐ Ⓑ Ⓒ Ⓓ

11. Ⓐ Ⓑ Ⓒ Ⓓ   36. Ⓕ Ⓖ Ⓗ Ⓙ

12. Ⓕ Ⓖ Ⓗ Ⓙ   37. Ⓐ Ⓑ Ⓒ Ⓓ

13. Ⓐ Ⓑ Ⓒ Ⓓ   38. Ⓕ Ⓖ Ⓗ Ⓙ

14. Ⓕ Ⓖ Ⓗ Ⓙ   39. Ⓐ Ⓑ Ⓒ Ⓓ

15. Ⓐ Ⓑ Ⓒ Ⓓ   40. Ⓕ Ⓖ Ⓗ Ⓙ

16. Ⓕ Ⓖ Ⓗ Ⓙ   41. Ⓐ Ⓑ Ⓒ Ⓓ

17. Ⓐ Ⓑ Ⓒ Ⓓ   42. Ⓕ Ⓖ Ⓗ Ⓙ

18. Ⓕ Ⓖ Ⓗ Ⓙ   43. Ⓐ Ⓑ Ⓒ Ⓓ

19. Ⓐ Ⓑ Ⓒ Ⓓ   44. Ⓕ Ⓖ Ⓗ Ⓙ

20. Ⓕ Ⓖ Ⓗ Ⓙ   45. Ⓐ Ⓑ Ⓒ Ⓓ

21. Ⓐ Ⓑ Ⓒ Ⓓ

22. Ⓕ Ⓖ Ⓗ Ⓙ

23. Ⓐ Ⓑ Ⓒ Ⓓ

24. Ⓕ Ⓖ Ⓗ Ⓙ

25. Ⓐ Ⓑ Ⓒ Ⓓ

1. If $\triangle ABC \sim \triangle DEF$, which correctly describes the relationship between the sides of $\triangle ABC$ and $\triangle DEF$?

A $\dfrac{DE}{AB} = \dfrac{FE}{CB}$

B $\dfrac{DF}{AB} = \dfrac{DE}{BC}$

C $\dfrac{BC}{DE} = \dfrac{AB}{EF}$

D $\dfrac{AC}{DE} = \dfrac{AB}{EF}$

2.

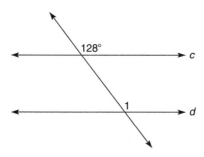

What is the measure of $\angle 1$ that makes line c parallel to line d?

F 52°

G 64°

H 128°

J 154°

3. Construct the bisector of $\angle ACD$.

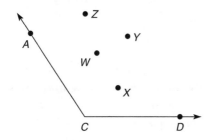

Which point lies on the bisector?

A W

B X

C Y

D Z

4. **Given:** $A(^-6, 1)$, $B(^-1, 5)$, $C(3, 2)$, and $D(^-2, ^-2)$.

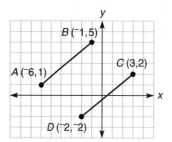

$\overline{AB}$ is parallel to $\overline{DC}$ because —

F the slopes are negative reciprocals of each other.

G the slopes are both equal to zero.

H the slopes are both undefined.

J the slopes are equal.

5. A bird feeder is placed on a board as shown below. If a board is placed parallel to the ground, what is the measure of the angle, x, that the board must make with the brace in order for the board to remain parallel to the ground?

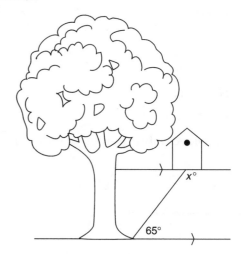

A 25°

B 65°

C 115°

D 155°

6. Construct ∠*MXY* with ∠*MXY* ≅ ∠*ZXY*.

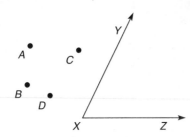

Which point lies on this angle?

F *A*

G *B*

H *C*

J *D*

7.

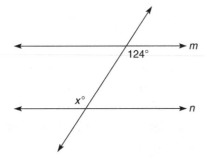

Find the value of *x* that makes *m* parallel to *n*.

A 56°

B 124°

C 146°

D 236°

8. A reflection of the point (8, 3) to (8, ⁻3) is the result of a reflection across the _?_.

F *y*-axis

G line *y* = *x*

H *x*-axis

J line *y* = ⁻*x*

9. Construct a line perpendicular to $\overrightarrow{BR}$ at *R*.

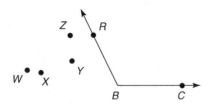

Which point lies on this perpendicular?

A *W*

B *X*

C *Y*

D *Z*

10. Which coordinates for *D* will make $\overline{CD}$ parallel to $\overline{AB}$?

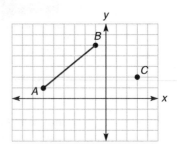

F (⁻2, ⁻2)

G (⁻2, 0)

H (⁻2, 2)

J (2, ⁻2)

11. A hexagonal floor has five congruent angles.

What is the measure of one of the congruent angles?

A 160°

B 116°

C 80°

D 44°

12. If a personal pan pizza (6-inch pizza) is cut into four equal slices, what is the area of one slice?

F $\frac{\pi}{4}$ sq in.

G $\frac{3}{2}\pi$ sq in.

H $\frac{9}{4}\pi$ sq in.

J 9π sq in.

13. The sum of the interior angles of a regular polygon is 3,960°. How many sides does this polygon have?

A 26 sides

B 24 sides

C 14 sides

D 12 sides

14. In this drawing, m∠D = 65°, m∠DCE = 40°, and ∠A ≅ ∠D.

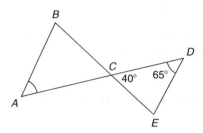

From shortest to longest, the sides of △ABC are —

F $\overline{BC}, \overline{AB}, \overline{AC}$

G $\overline{AC}, \overline{AB}, \overline{BC}$

H $\overline{AB}, \overline{BC}, \overline{AC}$

J $\overline{AB}, \overline{AC}, \overline{BC}$

15. The measure of the supplement of an angle is 60 degrees less than 4 times the measure of the complement of the angle. Find the measure of the supplement.

A 40°

B 50°

C 120°

D 140°

16. Find the sum of the measures of the exterior angles of a 7-gon.

F 360°

G 900°

H 1,080°

J 1,260°

17. **Given:** ∠1 ≅ ∠2 and ∠3 ≅ ∠4.

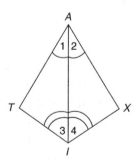

Which could be used to prove △TAI ≅ △XAI?

A (AAS) If two angles and a side not included are congruent to two angles and a side not included of another triangle, then the triangles are congruent.

B (SAS) If two sides and the included angle in one triangle are congruent to two sides and the included angle of another triangle, then the triangles are congruent.

C (ASA) If two angles and the included side of one triangle are congruent to two angles and the included side of another triangle, then the triangles are congruent.

D (HL) It the hypotenuse and a leg of one triangle are congruent to the hypotenuse and leg of another triangle, then the triangles are congruent.

18. From a point on a cliff 100 feet high, William sights his brother Edward in a boat at sea at an angle of depression of 7°.

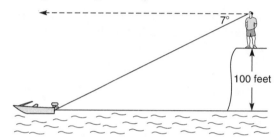

How far is Edward's boat from the base of the cliff?

F 820.6 ft

G 814.4 ft

H 100.8 ft

J 99.3 ft

19. **Given:** $\overline{DE} \parallel \overline{BC}$, AD = 3, AB = 10, and BC = 11.

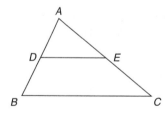

What is the length of $\overline{DE}$?

A 1.9

B 2.7

C 3.3

D 4.7

20. In the drawing, m∠X = 48° and m∠Y = 75°.

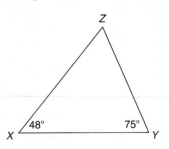

Which is the longest side of the triangle?

F $\overline{XY}$

G $\overline{XZ}$

H $\overline{WZ}$

J $\overline{ZY}$

21. One of the angles of a rhombus measures 120°. The perimeter of the rhombus is 32.

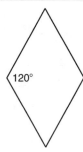

What are the lengths of the diagonals?

A 8 and $8\sqrt{3}$

B 8 and $8\sqrt{2}$

C 4 and $4\sqrt{3}$

D 4 and $4\sqrt{2}$

22. In order to cut out a regular hexagon from a piece of paper, what should be the measure of each angle of the hexagon?

F 135°

G 120°

H 60°

J 45°

23. A square and one of its diagonals are shown.

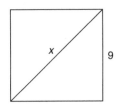

Find the value of x.

A $3\sqrt{2}$

B $3\sqrt{3}$

C $9\sqrt{2}$

D $9\sqrt{3}$

24. The length of a diagonal of a rectangle is shown with the given angle.

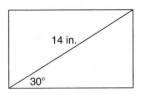

To the nearest tenth, what is the area of the rectangle?

F 69.3 sq in.

G 84.9 sq in.

H 138.6 sq in.

J 169.7 sq in.

25. Let p represent "A figure is a triangle."
Let q represent "The figure is a polygon."
What is the symbolic form of the statement, "If a figure is not a triangle, then it is not a polygon"?

A $\sim p \rightarrow q$

B $p \rightarrow q$

C $\sim q \rightarrow p$

D $\sim p \rightarrow \sim q$

26. Which conclusion logically follows the true statements?

"If I stay the night, then I will need extra money."

"If I go to the beach, then I will stay the night."

F If I do not go to the beach, then I will need extra money.

G If I do not stay the night, then I do not need extra money.

H If I go to the beach, then I will need extra money.

J If I stay the night, then I do not need extra money.

27. Given: ⊙O with $\overline{DT}$ as a tangent segment, DT = 16 feet, and AT = 8 feet.

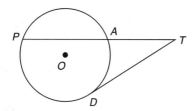

Find PT.

A 5 ft

B 9 ft

C 20 ft

D 32 ft

28. If WXYZ is a parallelogram, what are the co-ordinates of Y?

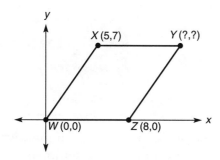

F (10, 7)

G (13, 7)

H (1, ⁻5)

J (⁻5, 1)

29.

What is the value of x?

A 155°

B 115°

C 65°

D 25°

30. Given: $m\widehat{PO}$ = 74° and $m\widehat{RT}$ = 22°.

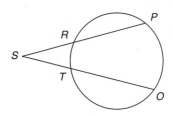

Find m∠S.

F 26°

G 48°

H 52°

J 96°

31. How much material is needed to cover the top of a cube with edges that are 6 centimeters long?

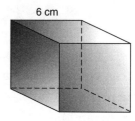

A 12 cm²

B 36 cm²

C 72 cm²

D 216 cm²

32. Which is the converse of the statement, "If two sides of a triangle are congruent, then the angles opposite these sides are congruent"?

F If two sides of a triangle are not congruent, then the angles opposite these sides are not congruent.

G If two sides of a triangle are congruent, then the angles opposite these sides are not congruent.

H If two angles of a triangle are not congruent, then the sides opposite these sides are not congruent.

J If two angles of a triangle are congruent, then the sides opposite these angles are congruent.

33. The tiling below is composed of equilateral triangles.

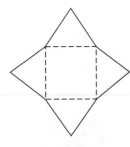

What is the value of x?

A 30°

B 60°

C 80°

D 120°

34.

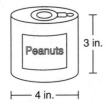

This net can be folded into a __?__ .

F square prism

G square pyramid

H triangular pyramid

J triangular prism

35. A can of peanuts has a diameter of 4 inches and height of 3 inches.

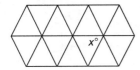

Find the volume of the can, to the nearest tenth of an inch.

A 18.8 cu in.

B 37.7 cu in.

C 56.5 cu in.

D 150.7 cu in.

36. Cylinder A is similar to cylinder B.

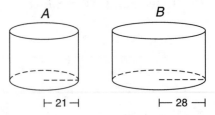

If cylinder A has a surface area of 216π, what is the surface area of cylinder B?

F 384π

G 288π

H 128π

J 64π

37. A jawbreaker is a piece of candy in the shape of a sphere.

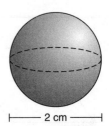

What is the surface area of the jawbreaker to the nearest tenth of a centimeter?

A 4.2 cm²

B 12.6 cm²

C 25.1 cm²

D 50.2 cm²

38. A cone has a radius of 3 and a height of 10. If the height is doubled and the radius remains the same, what effect does this have on the volume of the original object?

F The volume is 8 times greater.

G The volume is 6 times greater.

H The volume is 3 times greater.

J The volume is 2 times greater.

39. Which shows the front view of this figure?

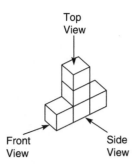

Top View

Front View Side View

A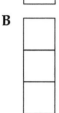

B

C

D

40. Find the distance between $A(5, 3)$ and $B(^-3, 1)$.

F 8.94

G 8.25

H 4.47

J 2.83

41. What type of symmetry does this figure have?

A Both horizontal and point symmetry

B Horizontal symmetry only

C Point symmetry only

D Vertical symmetry only

42. Mrs. Brown is designing a flower garden in the shape of a triangle. She knows that the lengths of two sides are 60 centimeters and 45 centimeters. What is a possible length for the third side of the flower garden?

F 110 cm

G 95 cm

H 10 cm

J 5 cm

43. The figure below has ? .

A line symmetry only

B point symmetry only

C no symmetry

D both line and point symmetry

44. The point $(5, ^-3)$ is rotated 90° counterclockwise around the origin. What are the coordinates of the image of this point?

F (3, 5)

G (3, $^-5$)

H ($^-3$, 5)

J ($^-3$, $^-5$)

45. Quadrilateral $ABCD$ is a parallelogram.

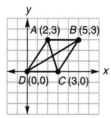

At what point do the diagonals intersect?

A $\left(\dfrac{^-5}{2}, \dfrac{^-3}{2}\right)$

B $\left(\dfrac{1}{2}, \dfrac{3}{2}\right)$

C (1, 3)

D $\left(\dfrac{5}{2}, \dfrac{3}{2}\right)$

Answer Sheet Sample Test B

Use a No. 2 pencil. Fill in the circle completely. If you erase, erase completely. Incomplete erasures may be read as answers.

1. Ⓐ Ⓑ Ⓒ Ⓓ
2. Ⓕ Ⓖ Ⓗ Ⓙ
3. Ⓐ Ⓑ Ⓒ Ⓓ
4. Ⓕ Ⓖ Ⓗ Ⓙ
5. Ⓐ Ⓑ Ⓒ Ⓓ
6. Ⓕ Ⓖ Ⓗ Ⓙ
7. Ⓐ Ⓑ Ⓒ Ⓓ
8. Ⓕ Ⓖ Ⓗ Ⓙ
9. Ⓐ Ⓑ Ⓒ Ⓓ
10. Ⓕ Ⓖ Ⓗ Ⓙ
11. Ⓐ Ⓑ Ⓒ Ⓓ
12. Ⓕ Ⓖ Ⓗ Ⓙ
13. Ⓐ Ⓑ Ⓒ Ⓓ
14. Ⓕ Ⓖ Ⓗ Ⓙ
15. Ⓐ Ⓑ Ⓒ Ⓓ
16. Ⓕ Ⓖ Ⓗ Ⓙ
17. Ⓐ Ⓑ Ⓒ Ⓓ
18. Ⓕ Ⓖ Ⓗ Ⓙ
19. Ⓐ Ⓑ Ⓒ Ⓓ
20. Ⓕ Ⓖ Ⓗ Ⓙ
21. Ⓐ Ⓑ Ⓒ Ⓓ
22. Ⓕ Ⓖ Ⓗ Ⓙ
23. Ⓐ Ⓑ Ⓒ Ⓓ
24. Ⓕ Ⓖ Ⓗ Ⓙ
25. Ⓐ Ⓑ Ⓒ Ⓓ

26. Ⓕ Ⓖ Ⓗ Ⓙ
27. Ⓐ Ⓑ Ⓒ Ⓓ
28. Ⓕ Ⓖ Ⓗ Ⓙ
29. Ⓐ Ⓑ Ⓒ Ⓓ
30. Ⓕ Ⓖ Ⓗ Ⓙ
31. Ⓐ Ⓑ Ⓒ Ⓓ
32. Ⓕ Ⓖ Ⓗ Ⓙ
33. Ⓐ Ⓑ Ⓒ Ⓓ
34. Ⓕ Ⓖ Ⓗ Ⓙ
35. Ⓐ Ⓑ Ⓒ Ⓓ
36. Ⓕ Ⓖ Ⓗ Ⓙ
37. Ⓐ Ⓑ Ⓒ Ⓓ
38. Ⓕ Ⓖ Ⓗ Ⓙ
39. Ⓐ Ⓑ Ⓒ Ⓓ
40. Ⓕ Ⓖ Ⓗ Ⓙ
41. Ⓐ Ⓑ Ⓒ Ⓓ
42. Ⓕ Ⓖ Ⓗ Ⓙ
43. Ⓐ Ⓑ Ⓒ Ⓓ
44. Ⓕ Ⓖ Ⓗ Ⓙ
45. Ⓐ Ⓑ Ⓒ Ⓓ

Sample Test B

1. In the figure below, lines *a* and *b* are cut by the transversal *t* forming the angles shown.

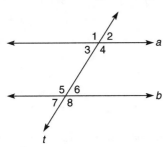

   Angles 1 and 8 are <u>?</u>.
   A corresponding angles
   B consecutive angles
   C alternate exterior angles
   D alternate interior angles

2. Why is $\overline{AB}$ parallel to $\overrightarrow{CD}$?

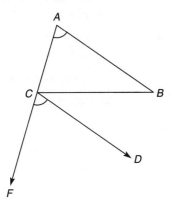

   F If two lines are cut by a transversal and alternate interior angles are supplementary, then the lines are parallel.

   G If two lines are cut by a transversal and consecutive (same-side) angles are congruent, then the lines are parallel.

   H If two lines are cut by a transversal and corresponding angles are congruent, then the lines are parallel.

   J If two lines are cut by a transversal and vertical angles are congruent, then the lines are parallel.

3. Which shows the bisector of segment $\overline{CD}$?
   A

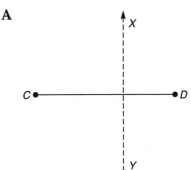

   B

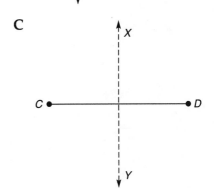

   C

   D

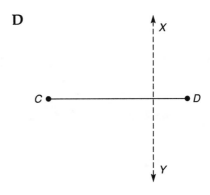

4. Find the value of *x* that makes line *n* parallel to line *m*.

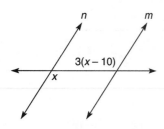

F 15°

G 30°

H 38.5°

J 52.5°

5. In the figure below, what is the value of *x*?

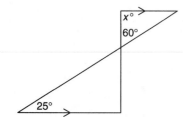

A 30°

B 65°

C 90°

D 95°

6. Construct a line perpendicular to $\overline{AC}$ from the point *B*.

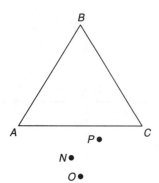

Which point lies on this perpendicular?

F *N*

G *O*

H *P*

J *Q*

7. **Given:** *C*(⁻3, 5), *D*(6, 4), and *W*(2, ⁻2),

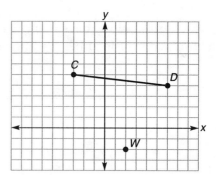

Which coordinates for *X* will make $\overline{WX}$ parallel to $\overline{CD}$?

A (⁻7, ⁻1)

B (⁻7, 1)

C (1, ⁻3)

D (7, 1)

8. A pair of vertical angles is supplementary. What can you conclude about the measure of the vertical angles?

F The vertical angles both measure 45°.

G The vertical angles both measure 60°.

H The vertical angles both measure 90°.

J The vertical angles both measure 180°.

9. What is the measure of ∠2 in the figure below?

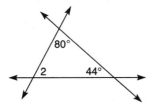

   A 44°

   B 56°

   C 90°

   D 100°

10. Why is $\overline{WZ}$ parallel to $\overline{XY}$?

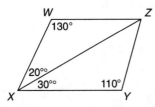

   F If two lines are cut by a transversal and vertical angles are congruent, then the lines are parallel.

   G If two lines are cut by a transversal and corresponding angles are supplementary, then the lines are parallel.

   H If two lines are cut by a transversal and same-side interior angles are congruent, then the lines are parallel.

   J If two lines are cut by a transversal and same-side interior angles are supplementary, then the lines are parallel.

11. Angle A is a complement of angle B. If m∠A = (8x + 14) and m∠B = (2x + 6), what is the value of x and the measure of ∠A?

   A x = 11, m∠A = 102°

   B x = 7.5, m∠A = 74°

   C x = 7, m∠A = 70°

   D x = 6, m∠A = 62°

12. In the drawing, the measure of ∠Z is 78° and the measure of ∠X is 23°.

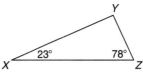

Not drawn to scale.

   Which is the longest side of the triangle?

   F $\overline{WZ}$

   G $\overline{XY}$

   H $\overline{XZ}$

   J $\overline{YZ}$

13. A guide wire on a light pole forms a 50° angle with the ground at a point 20 meters from the base of the pole.

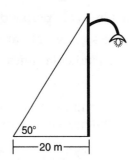

   What is the length of the guide wire, to the nearest tenth?

   A 12.9 m

   B 16.8 m

   C 26.1 m

   D 31.1 m

14. One base of a triangular prism has two sides that are 15 inches wide and 10 inches long. What is a possible length for the third side of the base?

   F 26 in.

   G 25 in.

   H 8 in.

   J 4 in.

15. Which is the inverse of the statement, "If Sharon cannot go, then Ruthie can go"?

   A If Sharon cannot go, then Ruthie cannot go.

   B If Sharon can go, then Ruthie cannot go.

   C If Ruthie cannot go, then Sharon can go.

   D If Ruthie can go, then Sharon cannot go.

16. Given: △*DMF* ~ △*GME*.

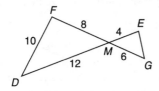

What is the length of $\overline{GE}$?

F 2

G 5

H 6

J 8

17. Which conclusion logically follows the true statements?

"Two perpendicular lines intersect."
"Two lines are not parallel if they intersect."

A Parallel lines are perpendicular.

B Two intersecting lines are perpendicular.

C Two perpendicular lines are parallel.

D Two perpendicular lines are not parallel.

18. A wheel chair ramp needs to be built as indicated in the drawing below.

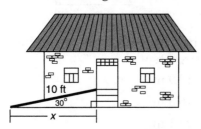

If the ramp is 10 feet long, what is the horizontal distance, *x*, from the end of the ramp to the porch?

F 5.0 feet

G 7.1 feet

H 8.7 feet

J 17.3 feet

19.

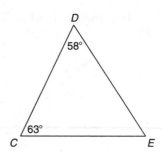

From shortest to longest, the sides of △*CDE* are ? .

A $\overline{CD}, \overline{CE}, \overline{DE}$

B $\overline{CE}, \overline{CD}, \overline{DE}$

C $\overline{CE}, \overline{DE}, \overline{CD}$

D $\overline{DE}, \overline{CE}, \overline{CD}$

20.

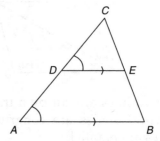

Which of the following correctly describes the relationship between the sides of △*ACB* and △*DCE*?

F $\dfrac{DE}{CE} = \dfrac{AB}{EB} = \dfrac{CD}{AD}$

G $\dfrac{DC}{EB} = \dfrac{AC}{DC} = \dfrac{DE}{AB}$

H $\dfrac{CE}{CB} = \dfrac{AB}{DE} = \dfrac{DC}{AC}$

J $\dfrac{AB}{DE} = \dfrac{AC}{DC} = \dfrac{CB}{CE}$

21. Steve travels 9 miles due north, 4 miles due west, 6 miles due north, and 12 miles due east. How far is Steve from his starting point?

A 12 mi

B 17 mi

C 18 mi

D 19 mi

22. Let *p* represent "A person lives in Richmond."
Let *q* represent "A person lives in Virginia."
Which is the symbolic form of the sentence, "If a person does not live in Richmond, then he does not live in Virginia"?

F $\sim p \rightarrow \sim q$

G $\sim p \rightarrow q$

H $\sim q \rightarrow \sim p$

J $\sim q \rightarrow p$

23. **Given:** $\overline{BD}$ bisects $\angle ABC$ and $\overline{AB}$ is congruent to $\overline{CB}$.

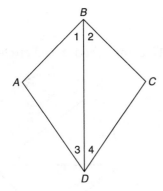

Which could be used to prove $\triangle ABD \cong \triangle CBD$?

A (SSS) If three sides of one triangle are congruent to three sides of another triangle, then the triangles are congruent.

B (SAS) If two sides and the included angle of one triangle are congruent to two sides and the included angle of another triangle, then the triangles are congruent.

C (AAS) If two angles and a non-included side of one triangle are congruent to two angles and a non-included side of the other triangle, then the triangles are congruent.

D (ASA) If two angles and the included side of one triangle are congruent to two angles and the included side of another triangle, then the triangles are congruent.

24. This tiling consists of squares and equilateral triangles.

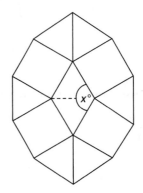

What is the value of *x*?

F 60°

G 90°

H 120°

J 150°

25. **Given:** Quadrilateral *KLJN* with $\angle N \cong \angle L$.

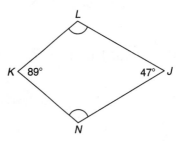

What is the measure of one of the congruent angles?

A 133°

B 112°

C 91°

D 90°

26. In the diagram below, *TRMV* is a quadrilateral with $\angle NVM \cong \angle RTV$ and $\angle VTM \cong \angle RMT$.

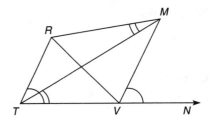

Why is *TRMV* a parallelogram?

F Both pairs of opposite sides are parallel.

G The angles are all congruent.

H The diagonals are congruent.

J The diagonals bisect the angles.

27.

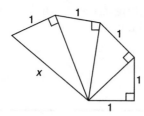

Solve for x in the diagram above.

A $\sqrt{37}$

B $\sqrt{6}$

C $\sqrt{5}$

D 2

28. *BOAT* is a square with its diagonals intersecting at point *X*.

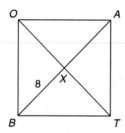

If $BX = 8$, the length of $\overline{TO}$ is ___?___.

F 4

G 8

H 12

J 16

29. The tiling below uses congruent hexagons.

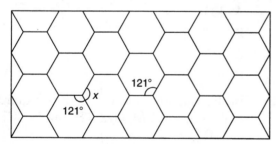

What is the value of x?

A 130°

B 121°

C 118°

D 116°

30.

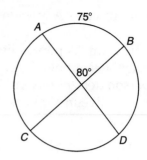

What is the measure of $\overset{\frown}{CD}$?

F 5°

G 10°

H 85°

J 95°

31. △*BAT* is inscribed in the circle below.

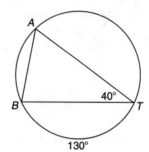

The measure of $\overset{\frown}{AT}$ is ___?___.

A 75°

B 80°

C 130°

D 150°

32. WXYZ is a rhombus with diagonals XZ and WY.

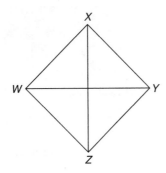

Which properties are true about the diagonals?

I   The diagonals are congruent.
II The diagonals are perpendicular.
III The diagonals bisect each other.
IV The diagonals bisect opposite angles.

F I and II

G I, II, and IV

H I, III, and IV

J II, III, and IV

33. $\overline{AD}$ is tangent to circle O.

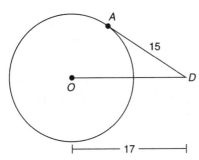

What is the length of the radius of circle O?

A 2

B 4

C 8

D 16

34. This net can be folded into which three-dimensional solid?

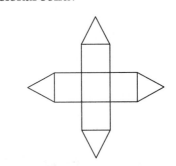

F

G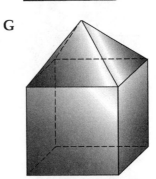

H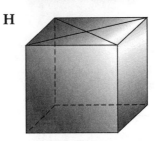

J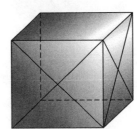

35. Identify the top view of this three-dimensional object.

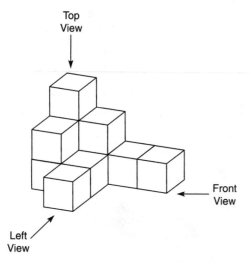

A
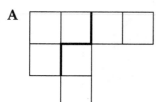

B
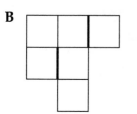

C
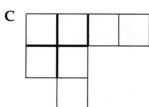

D
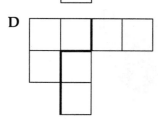

36. If the radius of a cylinder is doubled but the height remains the same, what effect does this have on the volume of the cylinder?

F The volume is 8 times greater.

G The volume is 6 times greater.

H The volume is 4 times greater.

J The volume is 2 times greater.

37. A cube is a rectangular prism with square faces.

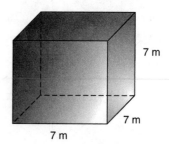

If each side is 7 meters long, the surface area is ? .

A 392 m²

B 343 m²

C 294 m²

D 196 m²

38. A rectangular container is 5 centimeters wide and 12 centimeters long and contains water at a depth of 8 centimeters. A roll of pennies is placed in the container and the water level rises by 2.1 centimeters. What is the volume of the roll of pennies?

F 2.1 cm³

G 126 cm³

H 482.1 cm³

J 606 cm³

39. The ratio of the volumes of two rectangular prisms is 64 : 27. What is the ratio of the heights?

A 64 : 27

B 16 : 9

C 8 : 3

D 4 : 3

40. What is the image of (3, 0) under a reflection over the *y*-axis?

F (⁻3, ⁻3)

G (⁻3, 0)

H (0, ⁻3)

J (0, 3)

41. The endpoints of a diameter of a circle are (⁻3, 0) and (0, 4). What is the length of the diameter of the circle?

A 1

B $\sqrt{7}$

C 5

D 7

42.

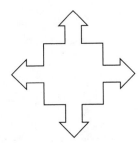

The figure has how many lines of symmetry?

F One

G Two

H Three

J Four

43.

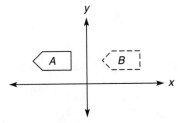

Pentagon *B* is —

A a reflection of pentagon *A* over the *x*-axis.

B a reflection of pentagon *A* over the *y*-axis.

C a translation of pentagon *A*.

D a 90° rotation of pentagon *A* around the origin.

44.

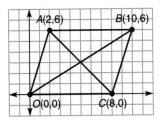

Quadrilateral *ABCD* is a parallelogram. At what point do the diagonals intersect?

F (5, 3)

G (4, 4)

H (3, 3)

J (⁻3, 3)

45.

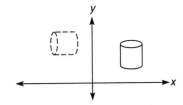

This drawing shows a —

A a reflection over the origin.

B a translation.

C a 90° rotation around the origin.

D a 180° rotation around the origin.

Answer Sheet Sample Test C

Use a No. 2 pencil. Fill in the circle completely. If you erase, erase completely.
Incomplete erasures may be read as answers.

1. Ⓐ Ⓑ Ⓒ Ⓓ
2. Ⓕ Ⓖ Ⓗ Ⓙ
3. Ⓐ Ⓑ Ⓒ Ⓓ
4. Ⓕ Ⓖ Ⓗ Ⓙ
5. Ⓐ Ⓑ Ⓒ Ⓓ
6. Ⓕ Ⓖ Ⓗ Ⓙ
7. Ⓐ Ⓑ Ⓒ Ⓓ
8. Ⓕ Ⓖ Ⓗ Ⓙ
9. Ⓐ Ⓑ Ⓒ Ⓓ
10. Ⓕ Ⓖ Ⓗ Ⓙ
11. Ⓐ Ⓑ Ⓒ Ⓓ
12. Ⓕ Ⓖ Ⓗ Ⓙ
13. Ⓐ Ⓑ Ⓒ Ⓓ
14. Ⓕ Ⓖ Ⓗ Ⓙ
15. Ⓐ Ⓑ Ⓒ Ⓓ
16. Ⓕ Ⓖ Ⓗ Ⓙ
17. Ⓐ Ⓑ Ⓒ Ⓓ
18. Ⓕ Ⓖ Ⓗ Ⓙ
19. Ⓐ Ⓑ Ⓒ Ⓓ
20. Ⓕ Ⓖ Ⓗ Ⓙ
21. Ⓐ Ⓑ Ⓒ Ⓓ
22. Ⓕ Ⓖ Ⓗ Ⓙ
23. Ⓐ Ⓑ Ⓒ Ⓓ
24. Ⓕ Ⓖ Ⓗ Ⓙ
25. Ⓐ Ⓑ Ⓒ Ⓓ

26. Ⓕ Ⓖ Ⓗ Ⓙ
27. Ⓐ Ⓑ Ⓒ Ⓓ
28. Ⓕ Ⓖ Ⓗ Ⓙ
29. Ⓐ Ⓑ Ⓒ Ⓓ
30. Ⓕ Ⓖ Ⓗ Ⓙ
31. Ⓐ Ⓑ Ⓒ Ⓓ
32. Ⓕ Ⓖ Ⓗ Ⓙ
33. Ⓐ Ⓑ Ⓒ Ⓓ
34. Ⓕ Ⓖ Ⓗ Ⓙ
35. Ⓐ Ⓑ Ⓒ Ⓓ
36. Ⓕ Ⓖ Ⓗ Ⓙ
37. Ⓐ Ⓑ Ⓒ Ⓓ
38. Ⓕ Ⓖ Ⓗ Ⓙ
39. Ⓐ Ⓑ Ⓒ Ⓓ
40. Ⓕ Ⓖ Ⓗ Ⓙ
41. Ⓐ Ⓑ Ⓒ Ⓓ
42. Ⓕ Ⓖ Ⓗ Ⓙ
43. Ⓐ Ⓑ Ⓒ Ⓓ
44. Ⓕ Ⓖ Ⓗ Ⓙ
45. Ⓐ Ⓑ Ⓒ Ⓓ

1. Find the measure of ∠*DEF* in the figure below.

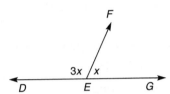

   A 135°

   B 120°

   C 60°

   D 45°

2. **Given:** Pentagon *ABCDF* with two right angles.

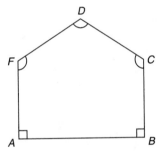

   If the remaining angles are all congruent, the measure of one of these angles is __?__ .

   F 90°

   G 108°

   H 120°

   J 140°

3. A sphere has a radius of 4. If the radius is doubled, what effect does this have on the volume of the sphere?

   A The volume is 10 times greater.

   B The volume is 8 times greater.

   C The volume is 6 times greater.

   D The volume is 4 times greater.

4. Construct the bisector of ∠*BOX*.

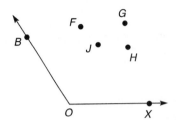

   This bisector passes through which point?

   F *F*

   G *G*

   H *H*

   J *J*

5. Which pair of angles must be congruent in order for line *a* to be parallel to line *b*?

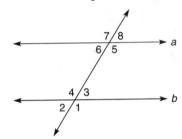

   A ∠2 and ∠3

   B ∠5 and ∠3

   C ∠7 and ∠1

   D ∠8 and ∠4

6. Find the perimeter of the figure below.

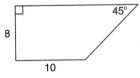

   F $28 + 8\sqrt{2}$

   G $28 + 8\sqrt{3}$

   H $36 + 8\sqrt{2}$

   J $36 + 8\sqrt{3}$

7. Given: $N(^-3, ^-2)$, $O(2, 4)$, and $P(6, 4)$.

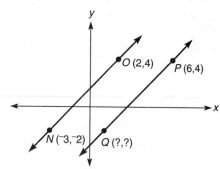

Which coordinates for Q will make $\overleftrightarrow{QP}$ parallel to $\overrightarrow{NO}$?

A $(1, ^-2)$

B $(^-1, ^-2)$

C $(^-2, 1)$

D $(^-2, ^-1)$

8.

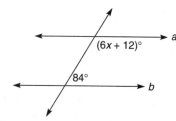

Line a will be parallel to line b when $x = $ __?__ .

F 12

G 13

H 14

J 16

9. Chords $\overline{WY}$ and $\overline{XZ}$ intersect at P.

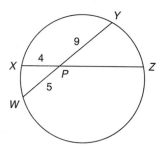

What is the length of $\overline{PZ}$?

A 2.22

B 7.20

C 11.25

D 17.50

10.

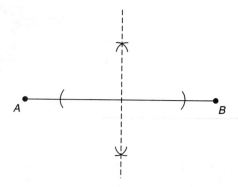

The drawing shows the arcs for the construction of —

F a segment congruent to a given segment.

G an angle bisector.

H a perpendicular bisector.

J a perpendicular to a line from a point not on the line.

11.

Which line is congruent to $2a + b$?

A ———

B —————

C ———————

D ——————

12.

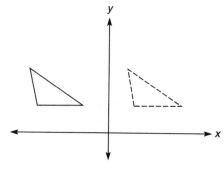

The drawing shows a __?__ .

F 90° rotation around the origin

G 270° rotation around the origin

H reflection over the y-axis

J translation

13. Let c represent "x is an even integer."
Let d represent "x is divisible by 2."
When x is 13, which of the following is true?

A $\sim c \wedge d$

B $\sim c \wedge \sim d$

C $c \wedge d$

D $c \wedge \sim d$

14.

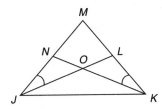

Which could be used to prove △*MJL* ~ △*MKN*?

F AA~

G ASA~

H SAS~

J SSS~

15. Given: Circle *O* with a radius of 10 and ∠*AOB* = 90°.

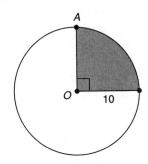

Find the area of the shaded region.

A 2.5π

B 5π

C 12π

D 25π

16. A 34 foot ladder is leaning on a wall as shown below.

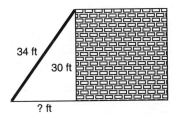

How far is the foot of the ladder from the wall?

F 4 ft

G 16 ft

H 26 ft

J 45 ft

17. Which pairs of triangles are similar?

I II III

A I and II

B I only

C I, II, and III

D II and III

18. Two similar prisms have heights of 10 and 25. If the volume of the larger prism is 750, what is the volume of the smaller prism?

F 48

G 120

H 240

J 300

19.

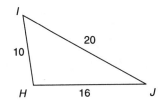

Which represents the angles from smallest to largest?

A ∠*I*, ∠*H*, and ∠*J*

B ∠*I*, ∠*J*, and ∠*H*

C ∠*J*, ∠*I*, and ∠*H*

D ∠*J*, ∠*H*, and ∠*I*

20. Given: $A(^-1, 2)$, $B(^-1, 5)$, $C(3, 2)$, $X(1, 4)$, $Y(1, 8)$, and $Z(4, 4)$.

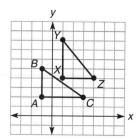

The two triangles are congruent. Which names the vertices in corresponding order?

F A and X; B and Y; C and Z

G A and X; B and Z; C and Y

H A and Y; B and Z; C and X

J A and Z; B and Y; C and X

21.

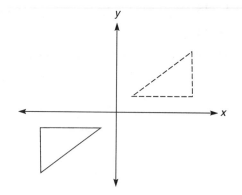

The drawing shows —

A a reflection.

B a reflection and a translation.

C a rotation.

D a translation.

22. Which conclusion do the following statements justify?

"If you pass the test, then you will be eligible to go on the trip."

"If you study hard, then you will pass the test."

F If you study hard, then you will be eligible to go on the trip.

G If you study hard, then you will pass the test.

H If you pass the test, then you studied hard.

J If you do not pass the test, then you will not be eligible to go on the trip.

23. A campsite is located at the base of each tree as shown in the figure below.

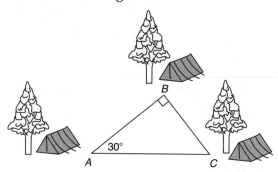

Which lists the distance between the campsites in order from least to greatest?

A AC, AB, and BC

B AC, BC, and AB

C BC, AB, and AC

D BC, AC, and AB

24. Given: $\overline{OR} \parallel \overline{TP}$ and m$\angle ROP = 30°$.

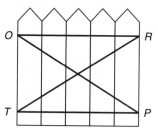

What is the measure of $\angle OPT$?

F 150°

G 60°

H 30°

J 15°

25. The measures of four of the angles of a pentagon are 90°, 120°, 95°, and 110°. What is the measure of the fifth angle?

A 185°

B 125°

C 85°

D 70°

26. Three vertices of a square are (2, 5), (2, $^-$1), (8, $^-$1). Find the coordinates of the fourth vertex.

F (8, 5)

G (5, $^-$8)

H ($^-$8, 5)

J ($^-$8, $^-$5)

27. Which can be the lengths of the sides of a triangle?

   A 9, 13, 23

   B 9, 12, 23

   C 9, 12, 14

   D 9, 10, 20

28. William wishes to carpet his rectangular patio, whose dimensions are 21 feet by 18 feet. How much will it cost William to cover his patio if the carpet costs $4.95 per square yard?

   F $1,871.10

   G $623.70

   H $311.85

   J $207.90

29. The tiling below consists of hexagons surrounded by regular triangles.

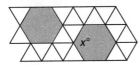

   What is the value of x?

   A 60°

   B 90°

   C 108°

   D 120°

30. **Given:** $\overline{PT}$ is tangent to circle O, $PT = 18$, $AB = 5x$, and $BT = 4x$.

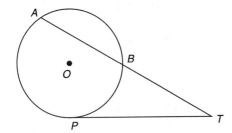

   The value of x is __?__.

   F 3

   G 4

   H 6

   J 9

31. **Given:** $m\widehat{OT} = (6x + 8)°$, $m\widehat{HG} = (2x)°$, and $\angle HIG = 84°$.

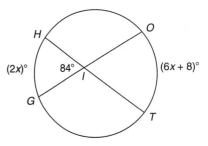

   Find the measure of $\widehat{HG}$.

   A 80°

   B 60°

   C 40°

   D 20°

32. Given quadrilateral $ABCD$ with $\overline{AB} \cong \overline{DC}$ and $\overline{AB} \parallel \overline{DC}$, why is $ABCD$ a parallelogram?

   F The diagonals bisect the angles.

   G The diagonals are congruent.

   H One pair of opposite sides is both congruent and parallel.

   J One pair of consecutive sides is congruent.

33.

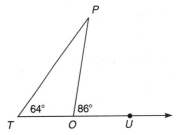

   What is the measure of $\angle P$?

   A 4°

   B 22°

   C 26°

   D 94°

34. Which net folds into a cube?

F

G

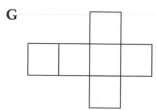

H

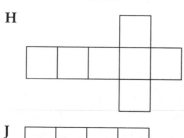

J

35. The volume of a cube is 64 cubic centimeters. What is the surface area of the cube?

A 4 cm²

B 16 cm²

C 64 cm²

D 96 cm²

36. In □ABCD, AB = 30 feet.

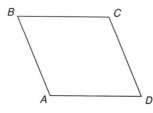

What is DC?

F 60 feet

G 30 feet

H 25 feet

J 15 feet

37. On a map, 1 centimeter represents 45 kilometers. If the distance between two cities is 315 kilometers, how far apart are they on the map?

A 5 cm

B 6 cm

C 7 cm

D 8 cm

38. A sandbox is constructed with dimensions 25 feet by 15 feet by 8 feet.

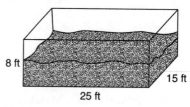

It the sand is only 5 feet high, what is the volume of the sand in the box?

F 1,250 cubic feet

G 1,875 cubic feet

H 2,000 cubic feet

J 3,000 cubic feet

39. In the figure below, which lines are parallel?

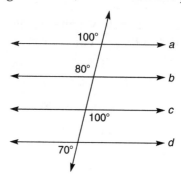

A b and d

B b and c

C a and d

D a and c

40. If the coordinates of A are (1, 0) and the coordinates of B are (2, 6), what are the coordinates of the midpoint of $\overline{AB}$?

F $\left(\frac{3}{2}, 3\right)$

G $\left(\frac{5}{2}, 3\right)$

H $\left(3, \frac{-3}{2}\right)$

J (5, 0)

41. Which figure has both point and line symmetry?

A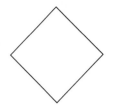

B

C

D

42. Which is the inverse of the statement, "If an angle measures 90°, then it is a right angle"?

F If an angle does not measure 90°, then it is not a right angle.

G If an angle is a right angle, then it measures 90°.

H If an angle is not a right angle, then it does not measure 90°.

J If an angle measures 90°, then it is not a right angle.

43. Given $X(^-3, 7)$ and $Y(4, 3)$, the distance between these two points is __?__.

A $\sqrt{149}$

B $\sqrt{101}$

C $\sqrt{65}$

D $\sqrt{17}$

44. The figure below has __?__.

F point symmetry only

G point and line symmetry

H line symmetry only

J no symmetry

45. A pilot flying over level ground at an altitude of 550 meters sights a marker. The angle of depression measures 10°.

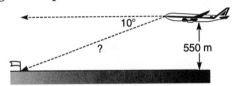

Find the distance between the marker and the plane.

A 96 meters

B 558 meters

C 3,119 meters

D 3,167 meters

Geometry Formula Sheet

Geometric Formulas

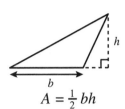

$A = \frac{1}{2}bh$

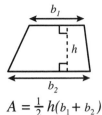

$A = \frac{1}{2}h(b_1 + b_2)$

$V = Bh$
$L.A. = hp$
$S.A. = L.A. + 2B$

$V = \frac{1}{3}Bh$
$L.A. = \frac{1}{2}lp$
$S.A. = L.A. + B$

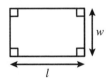

$A = lw$
$p = 2(l + w)$

$A = \pi r^2$
$C = 2\pi r$

$V = \pi r^2 h$
$L.A. = 2\pi rh$
$S.A. = 2\pi r(h + r)$

$V = \frac{4}{3}\pi r^3$
$S.A. = 4\pi r^2$

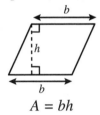

$A = bh$

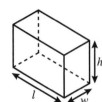

$V = lwh$
$S.A. = 2lw + 2lh + 2wh$

$V = \frac{1}{3}\pi r^2 h$
$L.A. = \pi rl$
$S.A. = \pi r(l + r)$

$c^2 = a^2 + b^2$

Geometric Symbols

Example	Meaning
$\angle A$	angle A
$m\angle A$	measure of angle A
$\overline{AB}$	line segment AB
AB	measure of line segment AB
$\overleftrightarrow{AB}$	line AB
$\triangle ABC$	triangle ABC
$\square ABCD$	rectangle $ABCD$
$\diagup\!\!\!\diagup ABCD$	parallelogram $ABCD$

Example	Meaning
$\overrightarrow{AB}$	vector AB
⌐→	right angle
$\overleftrightarrow{AB} \| \overleftrightarrow{CD}$	Line AB is parallel to line CD.
$\overleftrightarrow{AB} \perp \overleftrightarrow{CD}$	Line AB is perpendicular to line CD.
$\angle A \cong \angle B$	Angle A is congruent to angle B.
$\triangle A \sim \triangle B$	Triangle A is similar to triangle B.
	Similarly marked segments are congruent.
	Similarly marked angles are congruent.

Abbreviations

Volume	V
Lateral Area	L.A.
Total Surface Area	S.A.
Area of Base	B

Pi

$\pi \approx 3.14$

$\pi \approx \frac{22}{7}$

For further information, contact: Virginia Department of Education, Division of Instruction at http://www.pen.k12.va.us/VDOE/Instruction, or at P.O. Box 2120, Richmond VA 23218-2120.

Index